The Gig Economy
Cutting through the BS

Richard Lowe

The Writing King

The Gig Economy: Cutting through the BS

Table of Contents

See books by Richard Lowe at

https://masterofworlds.com

Get free publishing insights and industry updates at

https://thewritingking.substack.com

For ghostwriting and book coaching services see

https://thewritingking.com

Disclaimer

This book is for educational and informational purposes only and should not be considered specific financial, legal, tax, or business advice. The strategies, examples, and case studies presented reflect the author's personal experience and research, but your results will vary dramatically based on your individual circumstances, skills, market conditions, and how well you implement the ideas.

No income guarantees are made or implied anywhere in this book. The income figures and case studies represent specific situations and outcomes that are not typical results. Past performance doesn't guarantee future results, and all business ventures involve substantial risk of financial loss. You should never invest more than you can afford to lose or rely solely on this information for important business decisions.

Business structure, tax obligations, and legal requirements vary significantly by location and change frequently. This book doesn't constitute legal or tax advice, and you should consult qualified attorneys and accountants for guidance specific to your situation. The author isn't responsible for your compliance with local, state, or federal regulations.

The third-party platforms, services, and tools mentioned throughout this book may change their policies, fees, or availability without notice. The author has no control over these platforms and cannot guarantee their continued existence or functionality. Some mentioned services may involve affiliate relationships, and you should always verify current terms and conditions before using any service.

Market conditions can change rapidly and unpredictably. Competition increases, platforms modify their algorithms, economic factors shift demand, and what works today might not work tomorrow. Technology recommendations are based on current conditions and will become outdated. Security practices should be evaluated regularly and updated as technology evolves.

Working irregular hours, dealing with variable income, and managing business stress can seriously affect your physical and mental health. Your wellbeing is more important than any financial goal, and you should seek professional help if you experience persistent stress, anxiety, or other health issues related to work or finances.

This information is provided "as is" without warranties of any kind. The author disclaims all warranties and shall not be liable for any damages arising from the use of this information, including direct, indirect, incidental, consequential, or punitive damages. This limitation applies even if the author has been advised of the possibility of such damages.

You are solely responsible for your business decisions, financial outcomes, legal compliance, and personal safety. This book provides information and perspectives to help inform your decisions, but you must evaluate everything critically and make choices appropriate for your specific circumstances. Don't blame the author if things don't work out the way you hoped.

By reading this book, you acknowledge that you understand these limitations and agree to use the information at your own risk and discretion.

Preface

This book started as a money problem. I was trying to make enough to quit my soul-crushing office job without going broke in the process.

Like most people, I started by consuming every piece of advice I could find about making money online. I watched YouTube videos about passive income, bought courses about dropshipping, and tried to follow step-by-step blueprints that promised guaranteed success. I wasted months and hundreds of dollars chasing other people's strategies that didn't work for my situation.

The turning point came when I stopped trying to copy what worked for other people and started experimenting to find what worked for me. I began treating online income generation like a science experiment instead of following it like a religion. I tested ideas on a small scale, measured results honestly, and scaled what worked while abandoning what didn't.

That approach led me to ghostwriting, which became my primary income source and eventually allowed me to leave traditional employment entirely. But the real value wasn't in discovering ghostwriting specifically - it was in developing a methodology for finding opportunities that others miss and building systems that work with my brain instead of against it.

This book isn't a ghostwriting manual or a step-by-step guide to any specific income stream. It's the methodology I wish I'd had when I started: how to cut through the noise of conflicting advice, avoid the psychological traps that keep people stuck, and build sustainable income streams without burning out or compromising your values.

Most books on this subject fall into two categories: overly optimistic cheerleading that ignores real challenges, or pessimistic warnings that dismiss all opportunities as exploitation. This book takes a different approach. It acknowledges that building alternative income streams is difficult and risky while also recognizing that it's possible and potentially transformative for people who approach it strategically.

I'm not a motivational speaker or a business guru. I'm someone who figured out how to make this work through trial and error, documented what I learned, and decided to share it with people who are where I was twelve years ago. I've made most of the mistakes described in this book, which is why I can warn you about them with specificity rather than generalities.

The advice here is based on my experience as someone with ADHD who needed flexibility more than security, who valued autonomy more than predictability, and who was willing to trade the illusion of employment safety for the reality of self-directed income generation. Your priorities and constraints are probably different, which is why this book focuses on principles and methodology rather than specific tactics.

This isn't a get-rich-quick scheme or a promise of easy money. Building sustainable income streams requires work, patience, and the willingness to experiment with ideas that might not work out. But for people who are tired of trading time for money on someone else's terms, it offers a path toward something better.

Independent work has real problems: platform dependency, irregular income, lack of benefits, and predatory business models that exploit workers. This book doesn't ignore these problems or pretend they don't exist.

Instead, it shows how to navigate around them by building income streams that you control rather than income streams that control you.

If you're looking for validation that your current approach is perfect, this probably isn't the book for you. If you're looking for someone to promise that success is guaranteed if you just follow their system, you'll be disappointed. But if you're willing to experiment, learn from failures, and build something systematically over time, this book provides the framework for doing exactly that.

The methodology works, but only if you work it.

Introduction: Why I'm Qualified to Call BS

You've probably read a dozen books about making money online. Maybe you've tried a few of the "proven systems." Maybe you're wondering why you're still broke despite following all the expert advice.

I'm here to tell you why: most of it is complete garbage.

I should know. I've tried almost everything. Contest sites that pay pennies for hours of work. "Read for pay" schemes that amount to intellectual slavery. Games that promise rewards but deliver nothing. Fiverr gigs that had me competing with people willing to work for less than minimum wage. Dropshipping before automation ruined it. eBay arbitrage until fees killed the margins. Affiliate marketing until I couldn't sleep at night promoting garbage to make a buck.

I made $10,000 in affiliate marketing and walked away because the industry is filled with scammers and predators. I made $35,000 on eBay before shipping costs and platform fees made it unsustainable. I tested Etsy when it was still about handmade goods, before dropshipped junk from China buried every legitimate seller.

Here's what worked: I built a ghostwriting business that generates $150,000 a year. I publish my own books that bring in a few hundred dollars monthly in passive income. These aren't get-rich-quick schemes. They're sustainable income streams that get better with time instead of falling apart when the next algorithm change hits.

I'm ADHD, which means I've had to figure out how to build income streams that work with my brain, not against it. The hyperfocus, the need for variety, the inconsistent energy levels. I've learned to turn these into advantages.

This book isn't going to teach you to copy what I did. Ghostwriting is MY path, not THE path. I'm going to teach you the methodology I used to find what works: how to experiment with minimal risk, how to spot opportunities others miss, how to build multiple income streams so you're not dependent on any single platform or market.

I'm going to tell you what NOT to waste your time on. The micro-income traps. The platforms designed to exploit your labor. The scams disguised as opportunities. The MLM schemes that prey on desperation. I've tested this stuff so you don't have to.

I'm going to show you how to do this ethically and sustainably. How to practice good accounting from day one. How to avoid debt that will trap you in cycles of desperation. How to build something that improves your life instead of consuming it.

This can work. But not the way the gurus tell you it works. Not with their recycled advice and fantasy income projections. It works when you stop following everyone else's playbook and start building your own through smart experimentation and honest assessment of what's worth your time.

One more thing before we start. The job landscape is changing faster than most people are prepared for. Not a collapse, just a shift. The skills that made you valuable five years ago may need to be repositioned. The role you have today may look different in three years. Platforms and tools that don't exist yet will change how certain kinds of work get done. None of that is catastrophic if you're building income that doesn't depend entirely on one employer, one platform, or one skill set holding its value forever.

Building independent income while you're employed isn't a backup plan. It's the most practical thing you can do given how quickly conditions can change. The gap between people who navigate transitions smoothly and people who get caught unprepared is usually a few months of low-stakes experimentation started before anything went wrong. That's what this book is about.

Let's cut through the bullshit and get to work.

How to Use This Book

This book is over 60,000 words. Nobody reads that many words in the order they were written. Here's where to start based on your situation.

You just lost your job and need income within 30 days

Start with "If You Just Lost Your Job" at the beginning of Part II, which addresses your situation directly and lays out three tiers: survival work (need money today, zero runway), bridge work (stabilizes income while you build), and building work (what the rest of this book is about). If you have nothing in the bank, start at survival work and don't skip it. Then read "The Micro-Income Trap" and "The Race to the Bottom" in Part I so you know what not to waste time on. Read "Running It Like a Real Business" in Part III for honest timelines. Then go to "Your First 30 Days" at the end of the Conclusion and start. Come back to the rest later.

You're thinking about leaving your job but haven't yet

You have the best possible starting position: time and a paycheck. Read this book in order, but pay particular attention to "The Real Advantages and Disadvantages of Freelancing" in Part II, which is written for you. Build parallel income streams before you quit. The goal is to make your job optional before you make it gone.

You're employed and want a second income stream

Skip "If You Just Lost Your Job" since it's not your situation. Read Part I to understand what doesn't work, then go straight to "The Experimentation Method" in Part

II. That's the core of what this book is actually teaching. The methodology summary at the end of that chapter is the most important page in the book. Then read "Your First 30 Days" and start experimenting while you still have financial stability. Part III is reference material. Come back to it as you need it.

You've tried gig work and it hasn't worked

Read "The Mental Traps That Keep You Broke" in Part I first, not because you're being dumb, but because those patterns affect almost everyone and recognizing them explains a lot of why smart, motivated people stall. Then read "Why Copying Others' Exact Methods Usually Fails" in Part II. If either of those chapters describes what happened to you, the Experimentation Method that follows is the alternative. You probably don't need to read Part I's earlier chapters. You already know the traps.

You have limited time and want the core argument

About 90 minutes of reading: the Introduction, "The Micro-Income Trap," "The Affiliate Marketing Scam," "The Experimentation Method" (including the methodology summary at the end), "Your First 30 Days," and the Core Principles appendix. That's the spine of the book. Everything else is elaboration, evidence, or implementation detail. The Pro Tip and Danger Zone callouts scattered throughout are also worth scanning, as they carry most of the practical content in condensed form.

You're ADHD or neurodivergent

There's a full chapter written specifically for you in Part III: "Making It Work with ADHD and Neurodivergence."

Read it whenever it feels right. It doesn't depend on reading the rest first. The short version: the gig economy's flexibility and variety can work with a neurodivergent brain in ways traditional employment usually doesn't. The rest of the book applies to you too, but that chapter is where the specific strategies live.

You're retired or semi-retired and want supplemental income

You have something most readers in this book don't: time, experience, and no immediate financial emergency. That changes the calculus significantly. The urgency framing throughout this book isn't aimed at you, so skip it. What applies to you: the experimentation methodology, the skill arbitrage concept, and the platform dependency warnings.

Your path looks different from someone trying to replace a salary. You're not building toward quitting a job. You're building toward a few hundred or a few thousand extra dollars a month from something you can do on your schedule, using expertise you already have. Lower volume, higher margin, no hustle required.

Read "Examples, Not Blueprints" in Part II first. Petra's story is the closest to your situation: a skill that already existed, monetized locally, scaled only as far as she wanted. Rosa's story is also relevant. Then read the Experimentation Method with this question in mind: what do I already know that someone nearby would pay me for? The answer is probably more obvious than you think. Then read "Running It Like a Real Business" in Part III for the practical basics. Skip the ADHD chapter unless it applies. The Hardware and AI Tools chapters are in the appendixes. Come back to them when you need them.

One practical flag: supplemental income affects Social Security benefits and pension arrangements differently depending on your situation and jurisdiction. Before you start generating meaningful income, have a conversation with an accountant about how it interacts with whatever you're already receiving. It's usually manageable, but it's better to know the rules before you're surprised by them.

You're a creative: writer, artist, designer, photographer, musician

Most of Part I was written with you in mind, even if it doesn't say so. The race to the bottom on platforms like Fiverr, the devaluation of skills by global wage arbitrage, the affiliate marketing trap. These hit creatives harder than most because creative work is the first thing buyers try to commoditize. Read Part I, then read "The Race to the Bottom" section twice.

The skill arbitrage concept is the most relevant to you: finding the market where your skill is rare instead of the market where it's common. Most creatives are competing in the wrong market. The Ghostwriting case study in "Examples, Not Blueprints" is not about ghostwriting. It's about exactly that. The Petra sewing case study is equally applicable: a creative skill, tested locally, scaled toward the work clients actually asked for rather than the work she assumed they wanted.

The one thing this book won't do is tell you your creative work has inherent market value. It might. It also might not, or not yet, or not in the market you're currently in. The experimentation method is how you find out without spending years on the wrong answer.

You're skeptical and not sure this is for you

Good. Skepticism is appropriate, since most books in this category are selling a fantasy. Read Part I. If it matches your own experience with platforms and online income schemes, the rest of the book is probably worth your time. If it feels like I'm making excuses for why all the strategies failed rather than pointing you toward something real, stop. The Introduction explains what I actually made and how, and what I walked away from. Start there.

Part I: The Bullshit (What Doesn't Work)

This section is going to spend a lot of time on what doesn't work. That's intentional, and it's worth explaining why it comes first. Every trap in the next seven chapters is designed to look like an opportunity. The people running these schemes have studied what makes people try things, stay in things, and keep investing in things that aren't working. If you don't understand the mechanics of why these fail, you're likely to encounter them, try them, and waste months figuring out through experience what you could have understood in an hour of reading. More importantly: understanding exactly why something fails tells you precisely what would have to be different for something to succeed. The principles that make this actually work aren't arbitrary. They're the inverse of everything you're about to see go wrong.

Why Traditional Jobs Don't Cut It Anymore

Your grandfather could work at the same company for thirty years, get a pension, and retire with dignity. Your father could work at a company for fifteen years, get decent benefits, and have some job security.

You? You're lucky if your job lasts three years before the next "restructuring."

The social contract is broken. Companies stopped being loyal to employees decades ago, but we're still pretending the old rules apply. They'll lay you off the day before your benefits vest. They'll call you "family" while paying you just enough to keep you from quitting. They'll demand you be "passionate" about work that treats you like a replaceable cog.

The money is garbage. Salaries haven't kept up with inflation in decades. A "good" job that pays $50,000 a year barely covers rent in most cities. Meanwhile, your boss makes forty times what you make while telling you there's no budget for raises.

The benefits they dangle aren't even that good anymore. Health insurance with a $5,000 deductible isn't health insurance. It's catastrophic injury coverage with a monthly payment. "Unlimited PTO" means you'll feel guilty taking any time off. The 401k match disappeared when the market got bumpy.

Here's the real problem: you have no control. Your income depends entirely on someone else's mood, someone else's budget decisions, someone else's idea of what you're worth. They can cut your hours, freeze your salary, or eliminate your position whenever the quarterly numbers look bad.

You're trading time for money on someone else's schedule. Eight hours a day, five days a week, fifty weeks a year. Same cubicle, same commute, same meetings that could have been emails. If you're ADHD like me, this setup is torture. Your brain craves variety and you're stuck doing the same tasks until you want to crawl out of your skin.

The "security" is an illusion. There's nothing secure about depending on one source of income that can disappear with two weeks' notice. There's nothing secure about building skills that only matter to one employer. There's nothing secure about having your financial future tied to whether your boss likes you.

This isn't about being lazy or entitled. The game changed while we were still playing by the old rules. The companies figured out they could extract more value while giving less back. They're not going to start caring about employee welfare because you work harder or show more loyalty.

So what's the alternative? Building your own income streams. Creating value on your own terms. Developing skills that serve you, not just your employer. Having multiple sources of money so no single person or company can control your financial future.

Freelancing gets a bad rap because most people approach it wrong. They try to replace their job income overnight with Uber driving or TaskRabbit gigs. That's not what this is about. Build parallel income streams while you still have that steady paycheck. Create options so you're not trapped.

Your job isn't going away tomorrow. But your dependence on it can start ending today. And if it already went away (if you're reading this because you just got laid off), that changes the timeline, not the approach. This book is still for you.

Let me tell you about the first time I got excited about making money online. I found a contest site that promised $50 for writing a 500-word product review. Easy money, right? I spent three hours crafting the perfect review, submitted it, and waited.

Six weeks later, I got an email. I didn't win. The prize went to someone whose review was clearly written by a non-native speaker and probably cost them $2 on Fiverr to produce.

Welcome to the micro-income trap, where companies have figured out how to get quality work for almost nothing by dangling tiny carrots in front of desperate people.

Contests and Sweepstakes: The False Hope Factory

Contest sites are everywhere. Write a logo design for $25! Create a business plan for $100! Submit your best photo for $50! They make it sound like easy money, but here's how the math works:

You spend five hours on a logo design. Two hundred other people also spend five hours on logo designs. One person wins $25. Everyone else gets nothing. The company just got 1,000 hours of design work for $25. You just worked for free with a 0.5% chance of getting paid.

But your brain doesn't think about it that way. Your brain thinks about the $25 and ignores the probability. Casinos figured this out decades ago. Contest sites just applied the same psychology to labor.

I tried contests for three months. I won exactly once: $15 for a product name that took me two hours to research and develop. That's $7.50 an hour, which would be illegal if they were employing me.

Read-for-Pay: Intellectual Slavery

These schemes are insulting. "Get paid to read emails!" "Earn money reading articles!" "Make $200 a day just reading!"

Here's what they don't tell you: you're not getting paid to read. You're getting paid to click through advertisements, sign up for services, and provide your personal information to data brokers. The "reading" is just the wrapper around the real product, which is you.

I tried one that promised $0.02 per email. The emails were advertisements disguised as newsletters. To "prove" I read them, I had to click links, watch videos, and sometimes sign up for trial offers. After spending an hour clicking through garbage, I'd earned maybe $0.30.

But the real cost wasn't the time. It was what happened to my email address. Within weeks, I was getting hundreds of spam emails daily. My information had been sold to every scammer and marketer on the internet. I'd traded my privacy and sanity for thirty cents.

Games-for-Pay: The Dopamine Factory

"Play games and earn money!" sounds like a dream job until you realize the games are designed to waste your time, not reward it.

These apps use every psychological trick in the book. Bright colors, satisfying sound effects, variable reward schedules that trigger the same brain responses as gambling. You'll spend hours playing a match-three game to earn "coins" that convert to real money at laughably low rates.

I downloaded one that promised I could earn $50 for reaching level 100 in their puzzle game. Sounds reasonable, right? What they didn't mention was that the levels got exponentially harder and longer. Level 50 took me an hour. Level 75 took me three hours. By level 90, each level was taking me six hours, and I was spending real money on power-ups just to progress.

I never reached level 100. After two weeks of obsessive playing, I cashed out at level 87 for $12. I'd spent over forty hours playing a mediocre puzzle game for twelve dollars. That's thirty cents an hour.

Survey Sites: Data Mining Disguised as Research

"Share your opinion and get paid!" The survey sites make it sound like companies are dying to hear what you think about their products. They're not. They want your demographic data, your purchasing habits, and your contact information.

Most surveys disqualify you halfway through after they've already collected your data. "Sorry, you don't fit our target demographic!" But they keep the twenty minutes of personal information you just provided.

The surveys that do pay usually offer $0.50 for thirty minutes of your time. That's a dollar an hour. I've seen people defend this by saying "it adds up," but it doesn't add up to anything meaningful. You could make more money returning bottles to the grocery store.

Who's Really Profiting

Here's the dirty secret: these platforms aren't designed to make you money. They're designed to extract value from your time, attention, and personal information while giving you just enough reward to keep you hooked.

The contest sites get professional-quality work for pennies on the dollar. The read-for-pay schemes sell your data to advertisers and marketers. The game apps collect detailed behavioral data while serving you ads. The survey sites package your demographics and sell them to research companies.

You're not the customer. You're the product.

These companies have figured out how to monetize your desperation. They know people are struggling financially, so they create systems that feel like opportunities but are designed to extract maximum value while paying minimum rewards.

The platforms make millions. The advertisers get their data. The companies get their cheap labor.

You get carpal tunnel and a spam-filled inbox.

The Psychology of the Trap

Why do people fall for this? Because micro-income feels like progress when you're broke. Making $5 feels better than making nothing, even if it took you five hours. Your brain focuses on the money coming in and ignores the time going out.

These platforms are also addictive by design. They use the same psychological tricks as social media and gambling: variable rewards, progress bars, achievement badges, daily streaks. They're not paying you to work. They're paying you to get addicted to their platform so they can harvest your attention and data.

The saddest part is seeing people defend these schemes. "I made $20 last month!" they'll say, ignoring that they spent sixty hours to earn it. That's a thirty-three-cent hourly wage, but it feels like success because there's money in their account.

If you're going to spend time making money online, spend it on something that can scale. Something that gets easier and more profitable with experience. Something that builds skills you can use elsewhere.

Don't fall for the micro-income trap. Your time is worth more than thirty cents an hour, even if your bank account says otherwise.

I thought I was being smart when I joined Fiverr in 2018. "I'll write articles for $25 each," I told myself. "Easy money while I build my real business."

Three months later, I was writing 2,000-word articles for $10 because that's what it took to get orders. I was competing against writers in countries where $10 goes a lot further than it does in the U.S. I was trapped in a system designed to drive prices down to nothing.

Fiverr and platforms like it aren't marketplaces. They're race-to-the-bottom machines that pit desperate freelancers against each other while the platform collects a cut from every transaction.

Why $5 Gigs Keep You Poor

The name "Fiverr" tells you everything you need to know. Five dollars. That's what they think your skills are worth. Even when they expanded beyond $5 gigs, the mentality stuck. Everything is about being the cheapest option.

I watched graphic designers offering logo packages for $5. Logo packages that would cost $500 from a design agency. These weren't amateurs - these were skilled professionals who had been convinced that undercutting everyone else was a viable business strategy.

Here's the math that nobody talks about: Fiverr takes 20% of your earnings. So that $5 gig nets you $4. If it takes you an hour to complete (and it usually takes longer), you're making $4 an hour. If you live anywhere with a decent cost of living, you're working below minimum wage.

But it gets worse. The platform actively encourages buyers to demand revisions, additional work, and faster turnaround times. That $5 logo? The client wants three revisions, a business card design, and delivery within 24 hours. Now you're making $4 for six hours of work. That's 67 cents an hour.

The Global Wage Arbitrage Problem

The real issue isn't that people in other countries charge less. The real issue is that platforms like Fiverr create a system where geographic economics don't matter. A writer in Bangladesh can live comfortably on $300 a month. A writer in Los Angeles needs $3,000 a month just to survive.

When you're both competing for the same $25 writing gig, guess who's going to win? The person who can afford to bid $5.

This isn't about skill or quality. I've seen brilliant writers from expensive cities lose projects to mediocre writers from cheap countries purely because of price. The platform doesn't care about quality. It cares about transaction volume.

The buyers don't care either. They just want the cheapest option that meets their minimum requirements. Why pay $100 for excellent work when you can pay $10 for adequate work?

This creates a vicious cycle. As prices drop, quality workers leave the platform. As quality workers leave, the remaining workers feel pressure to drop their prices even further to compete.

Platform Dependency: Your Business Isn't Your Business

When you build your income on someone else's platform, you're building on quicksand. The platform can change its rules, adjust its algorithm, or eliminate your account without warning.

I watched this happen to a graphic designer who had built a six-figure business on Fiverr. He had hundreds of five-star reviews, regular clients, and a steady income. Then Fiverr changed their search algorithm. Overnight, his gigs went from the first page to the fifth page of search results. His orders dropped 90% in a month.

He tried everything. He lowered his prices, added new gigs, bought promoted listings. Nothing worked. The algorithm had decided his time was over, and there was nothing he could do about it.

That's the hidden cost of platform dependency. You think you're building a business, but you're building someone else's business. You're a sharecropper on digital land that you'll never own.

The Algorithm Controls Your Income

These platforms use algorithms to determine who gets seen and who doesn't. The algorithm considers response time, completion rate, customer reviews, and dozens of other factors that can change without notice.

Miss a few messages because you were asleep? Your response time drops and your gigs get buried. Get a few bad reviews from unreasonable clients? Your rating drops and your orders disappear. Take a vacation? Your completion rate suffers and you fall in the rankings.

You end up working around the clock, not because you want to, but because the algorithm punishes you for having a life. I knew freelancers who were afraid to sleep because they might miss a message and hurt their response time metrics.

The platform becomes your boss, except it's a boss that never explains its decisions and can fire you without cause.

Why Competing on Price Never Works

When price is your only competitive advantage, you have no competitive advantage. There will always be someone willing to work for less than you. Always.

I learned this the hard way. Every time I lowered my prices to win a project, I attracted clients who only cared about price. These clients were usually the worst to work with. They demanded the most revisions, paid the slowest, and left the worst reviews.

Meanwhile, the high-paying clients - the ones who cared about quality and had reasonable expectations - were working with freelancers who charged premium rates. These freelancers understood that good clients don't shop on price.

When you compete on price, you're signaling to the market that price is the most important thing about your service. You're training clients to see you as a commodity instead of a skilled professional.

The Hidden Costs of "Easy" Platforms

Fiverr and similar platforms market themselves as easy ways to start freelancing. Just sign up, create a gig, and start earning! What they don't mention are all the hidden costs:

The platform fee (20% on Fiverr) eats into every dollar you earn. The time you spend managing your profile, responding to messages, and dealing with platform politics is unpaid labor. The mental stress of depending on an algorithm for your income takes a real toll.

Then there are the opportunity costs. Every hour you spend grinding for $5 gigs is an hour you could spend building real client relationships, developing better skills, or marketing your services directly.

The worst hidden cost is what these platforms do to your self-worth. When you're constantly competing with people willing to work for pennies, you start to believe that's what your skills are worth. You internalize the platform's message that you should be grateful for any work at any price.

The Better Path

I'm not saying you should never use these platforms. They can be useful for getting experience when you're starting out. But they should be a stepping stone, not a destination.

Use them to build skills and collect testimonials, then get off as quickly as possible. Build direct relationships with clients. Create your own website. Set your own prices. Control your own business.

The goal isn't to win the race to the bottom. The goal is to avoid the race entirely.

Your skills are worth more than $5. Your time is worth more than competing with people willing to work for pennies. Don't let a platform convince you otherwise.

The internet is littered with the corpses of money-making opportunities that used to be gold mines. I should know - I rode several of them from boom to bust, watching easy money turn into impossible grinds as markets saturated and platforms evolved.

Knowing why opportunities die is just as important as finding new ones. Because whatever strategy is working now will eventually stop working, and you need to see the signs before you're the last person still flogging a dead horse.

eBay Arbitrage: Death by a Thousand Cuts

In 2015, I was making decent money buying stuff at garage sales and thrift stores, then reselling it on eBay. I'd find vintage electronics, brand-name clothes, and collectibles for a few dollars and flip them for $20-50. It was physical work, but the margins were solid.

Then eBay got greedy.

First came the fee increases. What started as a 6% final value fee crept up to 10%, then 12.35%, then 13.25% for most categories. But that wasn't the real killer - it was the shipping fee scam.

eBay started charging final value fees on shipping costs. So if I sold an item for $20 with $15 shipping, eBay would take their percentage of the full $35. They claimed this was to prevent people from gaming the system by charging $1 for the item and $34 for shipping, but the real reason was to squeeze more money out of sellers.

Then PayPal started holding funds for 21 days on new accounts, and sometimes longer for "high-risk" items. I'd sell something for $50, pay eBay their $6 fee immediately, but not get my $44 for three weeks. Meanwhile, I had to ship the item and pay for packaging and gas.

The shipping costs killed what was left. USPS prices went up every year, but customer expectations stayed the same. People expected free shipping, so I had to build shipping costs into my item prices. But then my items looked more expensive than competitors who were still charging separate shipping.

By 2018, I was spending $8 to list, package, and ship an item that sold for $25. After eBay's fees, I netted about $14. For something I bought for $5, that's a $9 profit - if nothing went wrong. One return or damaged package would wipe out the profit from three sales.

The final straw was when eBay started enrolling sellers in their "Managed Returns" program without asking. Buyers could return anything for any reason, and eBay would approve it. I had people return clearly used items claiming they were "not as described." I had buyers return expensive electronics after using them for weeks.

I quit eBay arbitrage when I realized I was making less per hour than I would at McDonald's, with way more stress and overhead.

Dropshipping: From Gold Rush to Automated Wasteland

Dropshipping used to be a real business model. In 2014, you could find products on Alibaba, create simple websites, and run Facebook ads to customers who didn't know they could buy the same stuff directly from China for half the price.

The margins were insane. I'd find a phone case that cost $2 from the supplier and sell it for $19.99. The supplier would ship directly to the customer, and I'd pocket $17 without ever touching the product. It felt like free money.

Then everyone discovered dropshipping.

YouTube exploded with "Dropshipping Millionaire" videos. Courses started selling for thousands of dollars. Every teenager with a laptop thought they could quit school and become an entrepreneur by copying products from AliExpress to Shopify.

The market got flooded. Every product that was profitable on Monday had fifty new competitors by Friday. Facebook ad costs skyrocketed as thousands of new advertisers bid against each other for the same customers.

But the real death blow was automation. Companies started creating tools that would import thousands of products from Alibaba to Shopify stores. People were launching "stores" with 10,000 random products they'd never seen, letting software handle everything from pricing to customer service.

These automated stores had no overhead, no quality control, and no shame. They'd undercut real businesses by selling the same products at cost, making their money from volume and payment processing delays.

The customers caught on too. Everyone learned to reverse-image search products to find the original supplier. Browser extensions started showing people the AliExpress price while they shopped on dropshipping sites. The information gap that made dropshipping profitable disappeared.

By 2019, dropshipping had turned into a scam playground. The only people making money were the course sellers teaching other people how to lose money dropshipping.

Etsy: From Handmade Haven to Chinese Sweatshop

Etsy used to be special. It was a place where real artists and craftspeople could sell genuinely handmade items to people who valued creativity and quality over mass production.

I had friends who made decent livings selling handmade jewelry, custom art, and vintage finds on Etsy. The platform promoted the "handmade" brand and customers paid premium prices for unique items.

Then Etsy went public and everything changed.

The company needed growth to satisfy shareholders, so they relaxed their handmade requirements. "Handmade" could include items that were "designed by the seller" even if they were manufactured in factories. Then it expanded to include "craft supplies" and "vintage" items.

The floodgates opened. Chinese manufacturers started flooding Etsy with mass-produced garbage marketed as "handmade." Search for "handmade necklace" and you'd get pages of identical items from different sellers, all shipped from the same factory in Guangzhou.

Real artisans couldn't compete. Why would someone pay $30 for a genuinely handmade bracelet when they could get something that looked similar for $3? The customers couldn't tell the difference from thumbnail photos, and Etsy's search algorithm started favoring cheap, high-volume sellers over quality craftspeople.

Etsy's fees went up too. They added payment processing fees, advertising fees, and transaction fees on top of listing fees. A small seller could easily lose 10-15% of their revenue to platform fees alone.

The final insult was when Etsy started pushing their own advertising platform. Sellers who didn't pay for ads got buried in search results. The platform that was supposed to level the playing field for small artists turned into another pay-to-play advertising auction.

The Lifecycle of Online Opportunities

Every online money-making opportunity follows the same predictable pattern:

Discovery Phase: A few smart people figure out a way to make money that others haven't noticed yet. Margins are high, competition is low, and early adopters get rich.

Growth Phase: Word spreads and more people enter the market. There's still money to be made, but you have to work harder for it. Competition increases but the market is still growing.

Maturation Phase: The opportunity becomes well-known. Everyone and their brother is trying to get in. Profit margins shrink as competition intensifies. Only the most efficient operators make decent money.

Saturation Phase: The market becomes oversaturated. Too many sellers chasing too few buyers.

Prices drop, quality suffers, and customer trust erodes. Most participants lose money.

Enshittification Phase: The platform starts squeezing users to maximize shareholder value. Fees go up, policies favor big players, and the user experience gets worse while profits get extracted upward.

Death Phase: The opportunity becomes a joke. Only scammers and course sellers remain, trying to extract money from newcomers who don't realize the party ended years ago.

This cycle happens faster now because information spreads instantly. What used to take years now happens in months. A profitable Amazon niche can go from discovery to death in six months if it gets featured in the right YouTube video.

How to Spot a Dying Opportunity

There are warning signs that an opportunity is heading toward saturation:

YouTube is flooded with "How I Made $10K" videos about that strategy. When every influencer is teaching the same method, it's too late.

The barrier to entry keeps getting lower. When something that used to require skill and effort becomes "automated" or "turnkey," it's about to die.

The platform starts changing rules frequently. When platforms keep adjusting their policies, algorithms, or fee structures, they're usually trying to manage oversaturation or extract more value from users.

Your profit margins keep shrinking despite working harder. When you're doing more work for less money, the opportunity is being commoditized.

New competitors appear constantly. When you can't keep track of all the new people entering your market, the market is getting ready to collapse.

Why Yesterday's Gold Rush is Today's Ghost Town

People get emotionally attached to strategies that used to work. They keep trying to optimize dead opportunities instead of looking for new ones. I watched eBay sellers spend years tweaking their listings and lowering prices, trying to recapture profits that were never coming back.

The internet rewards early adopters and punishes late adopters. By the time everyone knows about an opportunity, it's over for everyone except the people who got in early and built sustainable advantages.

This isn't anyone's fault. It's just how markets work. When something becomes easy and accessible, it stops being profitable. The money moves to wherever the next barrier to entry is highest.

The key is recognizing when you're fighting yesterday's war with today's weapons. Sometimes the best business decision is to walk away from something that used to work and find something that works now.

Your ego will tell you to keep trying. Your bank account will tell you to move on. Listen to your bank account.

I made $10,347 in affiliate marketing over eight months in 2017. Every guru would tell you that's proof the system works. Here's what they won't tell you: I hated every dollar of it.

Affiliate marketing isn't a business model. It's a pyramid scheme with better marketing. The people at the top make money selling dreams to the people at the bottom, who make money selling those same dreams to even more people at the bottom. The products? Nobody cares if they work.

How I Made $10,000 and Why I Walked Away

I got into affiliate marketing because it seemed logical. Find products you believe in, recommend them to people who might want them, earn a commission if they buy. Simple. Honest. Win-win for everyone.

I started promoting productivity software, online courses, and business tools. Stuff I used and liked. I wrote honest reviews, created helpful tutorials, and built a small but engaged audience. My commissions started at $200 a month, then $500, then over $1,000.

The money felt good. Easy money. Passive income. All the buzzwords that make broke people excited.

But the pressure to promote more products was constant. Every affiliate program wanted you to push harder, promote more often, drive more sales. The products that paid the highest commissions were usually the ones with the worst value propositions.

I started getting pitches for products I'd never heard of. Weight loss pills that "doctors don't want you to know about." Get-rich-quick schemes disguised as investment opportunities. Software that promised to automate your entire business for $97.

The affiliate managers were pushy salespeople who cared about one thing: volume. They'd send me swipe copy (pre-written promotional emails) that made ridiculous claims. "This product changed my life!" "I went from broke to millionaire in 90 days!" "Limited time offer expires at midnight!"

I refused to promote garbage, but I watched other affiliates make ten times what I made by promoting anything that paid well. They didn't care if the products worked. They cared if the products sold.

Then I realized what I was doing. I was building someone else's business using my audience's trust. The product creators got customers. The affiliate networks got transaction fees. I got a small percentage while taking all the reputational risk.

If a product I promoted turned out to be garbage, my audience blamed me, not the product creator. If someone got scammed by a course I recommended, they lost trust in me, not the course creator. I was the face of every transaction, but I had no control over the quality.

The final straw came when I promoted a $2,000 online course about building passive income. The course was garbage - recycled content you could find free on YouTube. But it had a great sales page and paid 50% commission.

Three people bought it based on my recommendation. One of them was a single mother who maxed out her credit card to pay for it. When she realized the course was worthless and asked for a refund, the course creator refused. Their "money-back guarantee" had so many loopholes it was meaningless.

I refunded her $1,000 out of my own pocket and stopped promoting affiliate products the next day.

The Ethics Problem: Promoting Garbage to Make Money

The affiliate marketing industry runs on a fundamental ethical problem: the people promoting products have no responsibility for the quality of those products. They're paid to drive sales, not to ensure customer satisfaction.

This creates twisted incentives. The products that pay the highest commissions are usually the ones with the highest margins, which usually means the lowest value. A $2,000 course with $2 worth of content can afford to pay $1,000 in affiliate commissions. A $50 course with $50 worth of content can only afford to pay $10.

Affiliates learn to promote based on commission rates, not product quality. They become salespeople for companies they've never worked with, selling products they've never used, to audiences they don't understand.

The successful affiliates learn to separate their emotions from their promotions. They'll promote weight loss pills on Monday, cryptocurrency courses on Tuesday, and real estate seminars on Wednesday. They don't care if any of it works - they care if any of it sells.

I watched affiliates promote products they knew were scams because the commission was too good to pass up. They'd write reviews claiming they "tested" products they'd never bought. They'd create fake before-and-after photos. They'd invent success stories about products that had never worked for anyone.

The justification was always the same: "I'm just showing people what's available. They can make their own decisions." But they weren't showing people what was available - they were showing people a carefully curated selection of high-commission garbage designed to extract maximum money from desperate buyers.

The Fake Income Machine

The whole system runs on manufactured social proof. Sales pages are covered with testimonials from people who supposedly made thousands using whatever is being sold. Most are fiction. I knew affiliates with templates for editing PayPal screenshots: a $500 month becomes $50,000 with thirty seconds of browser developer tools. They'd photoshop bank statements. They'd pay actors to record video testimonials about products they'd never used.

The guru culture made it structural. A guy who made $1,000 claimed $10,000. A guy who made $10,000 claimed $100,000. Those inflated numbers became the baseline. When someone honestly reported $500 their first month, it looked like failure. So they bought more courses. The failure was designed in.

Here's what the gurus don't say: most of them don't make their money from affiliate marketing. They make it selling courses about affiliate marketing. The math is obvious once you see it. A $2,000 course with a 50% affiliate commission can pay more per sale than months of promoting other people's products. So they run a few affiliate campaigns, document the results, and sell a course about the system. The course earns more than the affiliate marketing ever did. Their students are learning a business model the teacher already abandoned.

The industry is also structured to attract people who can't build real businesses but can write persuasive sales copy. Plausible deniability is built in: when a product turns out to be garbage, the affiliate says they don't control quality. The affiliate networks don't care. They care about volume.

The Real Cost of Affiliate Marketing

The biggest cost of affiliate marketing isn't the time or money you invest. It's what it does to your relationship with your audience.

When you become an affiliate marketer, you stop being a trusted advisor and become a salesperson. Every piece of content you create becomes suspect. Did you recommend that product because it's good, or because it pays well?

Your audience starts to notice. They become skeptical of your recommendations. They start to feel like they're being sold to instead of helped. The trust that took years to build can be destroyed in months.

I've seen content creators lose half their audience after going heavy into affiliate marketing. The people who stick around are usually the ones who buy everything, which means you end up with an audience of customers instead of an audience of fans.

The personal cost is even higher. You start to see everything through the lens of "can I monetize this?" You stop creating content to help people and start creating content to drive sales. Your passion project becomes a sales funnel.

I walked away from affiliate marketing because I realized it was changing me into someone I didn't want to be. Someone who would compromise their integrity for money. Someone who would exploit their audience's trust for commissions.

The $10,000 I made wasn't worth what I was becoming.

If you want to make money online, build something you can be proud of. Create real value for real people. Solve problems. Don't become another predator in an industry full of them.

Your audience deserves better. And so do you.

Every scheme in the first section of this book works because of patterns in how your brain handles uncertainty, loss, and social information. Contest sites exploit the same psychology as slot machines. MLMs exploit the same wiring that makes us trust people who seem confident. Platform dependency works partly because loss feels twice as bad as equivalent gain, so we keep doubling down instead of walking away.

The people running these schemes didn't study psychology out of academic interest. They studied it because it works. And the same patterns that make you vulnerable to external manipulation also show up in decisions you make entirely on your own: staying too long in something that isn't working, seeing what you want to see in early results, trusting experts who aren't.

The seven patterns in this chapter are the ones that have cost me the most money and time over twelve years. I'm not going to trace them back to evolutionary psychology. I'm going to show you what they look like when they're burning your cash.

Sunk Cost Fallacy: Why People Stick with Failing Strategies

"I've already spent six months learning dropshipping, I can't quit now." "I've invested $2,000 in this course, I need to make it work." "I've been working on this YouTube channel for two years, giving up now would waste all that effort."

These statements sound reasonable, but they're based on flawed thinking. The time and money you've already spent are gone regardless of what you do next. The only question that matters is whether continuing will be more profitable than switching to something else.

> ■ **Danger Zone:** The more you've invested in something, the harder it becomes to evaluate it objectively. Your brain wants to justify past decisions by continuing them, even when continuation is irrational.

I fell into this trap with affiliate marketing. I spent three months learning the business, building websites, and creating content. When I calculated my effective hourly rate after three months, it was $4.50. But instead of switching to something more profitable, I kept thinking "I just need to stick with it longer to see results."

I wasted another three months trying to make affiliate marketing work because I couldn't psychologically accept that my initial investment was a loss. By the time I finally quit, I could have learned ghostwriting and started making good money.

The antidote to sunk cost fallacy is setting clear criteria for success and failure before you start any new venture. Decide in advance how much time and money you're willing to invest, what results would indicate success, and what results would indicate it's time to quit.

Write these criteria down and refer to them when you're tempted to continue something that isn't working. Your future self will be more emotional and less objective than your current self, so make decisions when you're thinking clearly.

> ★ **Pro Tip:** Before starting any new income stream, write down exactly what would convince you to quit. Having exit criteria in advance prevents the sunk cost fallacy from trapping you in bad situations.

Also beware of the sunk cost fallacy in course purchases and coaching programs. The fact that you paid $2,000 for a course doesn't mean the information is valuable or that you should follow the advice. Evaluate strategies based on current evidence, not past purchase prices.

Confirmation Bias: Seeking Information That Supports What You Want to Believe

When you're excited about a potential income stream, your brain becomes a lawyer arguing for your predetermined conclusion rather than a scientist testing a hypothesis. You notice success stories and ignore failure rates. You remember the positive testimonials and forget the negative reviews.

Social media algorithms make confirmation bias worse by showing you content similar to what you've already engaged with. If you watch one video about cryptocurrency trading, YouTube will show you dozens more videos about people getting rich from crypto. You'll be flooded with "proof" that crypto trading works while never seeing content about people who lose money.

I experienced this when researching online course creation. I followed several successful course creators on social media and consumed content about course marketing, launch strategies, and income potential. My information diet was completely biased toward positive course creation content.

I didn't seek out information about course creation failure rates, the amount of work required to create good courses, or the challenges of building an audience. When I finally tried course creation, reality was much harder than my research had suggested.

> ▲ **Caution:** Information sources that profit from your participation (courses, platforms, affiliate marketers) have incentives to emphasize positives and downplay negatives. Seek out neutral sources and contrarian viewpoints.

Combat confirmation bias by actively seeking disconfirming evidence. For every success story you read, look for failure stories in the same field. For every positive review, read negative reviews. For every "this strategy works" article, find "this strategy doesn't work" articles.

Ask skeptical questions: What could go wrong? What are the failure rates? What hidden costs or challenges aren't being discussed? What qualifications or advantages do successful people have that I might not have?

Join communities where people discuss failures and challenges, not just successes. Reddit communities, Facebook groups for former MLM participants, and forums where people share honest experiences rather than promotional content.

Social Proof: Following the Crowd Off the Cliff

In this space, social proof manifests as people flocking to whatever opportunity seems popular at the moment. When everyone is talking about dropshipping, people start dropshipping businesses. When cryptocurrency trading is trending, people start day trading. When influencers promote affiliate marketing, people start affiliate marketing businesses.

The problem is that popularity doesn't indicate profitability. Often, the most popular opportunities are the least profitable because they're oversaturated with people who joined because of social proof.

By the time an opportunity is popular enough to create strong social proof, the early advantages have usually disappeared. The first people to sell on Amazon had little competition. The first YouTubers could get views easily. The first people in any trend benefit from low competition that later entrants don't enjoy.

> ★ **Pro Tip:** If there are multiple YouTube channels teaching "the exact system" for making money in a specific niche, that niche is probably already overcrowded.

Social proof also works through testimonials and success stories. When you see dozens of people claiming they made money with a particular strategy, your brain interprets this as evidence that the strategy works. But testimonials are not representative data.

Companies and course creators carefully select the most impressive success stories while hiding the failure stories. They might have 10,000 customers but only show testimonials from the 50 who got exceptional results. This creates a false impression of typical outcomes.

I was influenced by social proof when considering freelance writing platforms. I saw numerous success stories from writers making good money on Upwork and similar platforms. What I didn't see were the stories from writers who struggled to get clients, competed on price instead of value, or never made more than minimum wage.

The reality was that successful freelance writers on platforms were a small minority, but their visible success created social proof that influenced many others to try the same approach.

Resist social proof by focusing on base rates and representative data rather than cherry-picked success stories. What percentage of people who try this opportunity actually succeed? What do typical results look like, not just the best results?

Look for information about failure rates, average outcomes, and time-to-profitability. These data points are harder to find because they're less exciting to share, but they're more useful for making realistic decisions.

Authority Bias: Believing Experts Who Aren't Actually Experts

This world is full of fake authorities who use the trappings of expertise to sell products and services. They have professional websites, impressive-sounding titles, and polished marketing materials. They speak confidently about strategies and outcomes. They position themselves as successful entrepreneurs sharing their secrets.

But many of these "experts" make more money selling courses than they ever made from the strategies they teach. Their expertise is in marketing and sales, not in the business models they're promoting.

Real expertise comes from sustained success doing the work, not from teaching others how to do the work. A ghostwriter who's been making six figures for five years has more credible expertise than someone who wrote one successful piece and now sells a course about ghostwriting success.

I was influenced by authority bias when I bought a course from someone who claimed to be a successful Amazon seller. His sales page showed impressive income screenshots and detailed knowledge of Amazon's platform. His bio mentioned years of e-commerce experience.

Later I discovered that his main business was selling courses about Amazon selling, not actually selling products on Amazon. His "expertise" was in course marketing, not e-commerce. The strategies he taught were outdated or ineffective, but his authoritative presentation made them seem credible.

Combat authority bias by investigating the source of someone's claimed expertise. How long have they been doing the work they're teaching? What percentage of their income comes from the work versus teaching about the work? Can they provide verifiable evidence of sustained success?

Look for people who are still actively doing the work they teach about, not people who did it briefly and then shifted to teaching. Active practitioners understand current market conditions and practical challenges that former practitioners might not.

Ask for specific, verifiable evidence rather than accepting general claims about success. Anyone can create impressive-looking income screenshots or claim years of experience. Fewer people can provide detailed, verifiable proof of sustained success.

Loss Aversion: Why Bad Investments Get Worse

In the context of income streams, loss aversion manifests in two dangerous ways: avoiding good opportunities because they involve risk, and continuing bad investments to avoid realizing losses.

People often stick with low-paying, secure work instead of pursuing potentially higher-paying opportunities because the fear of losing their current income outweighs the potential gains from new income streams. They know their current situation isn't great, but it's familiar and predictable.

Loss aversion also makes people throw good money after bad investments. When something isn't working, the prospect of "losing" the money already invested feels worse than the prospect of gaining money from a new opportunity. So they keep investing in failing strategies to avoid the psychological pain of admitting failure.

I experienced this with a failed e-commerce business. After investing $3,000 in inventory and several months of work, the business was clearly not profitable. But instead of cutting my losses and trying something else, I invested another $2,000 trying to make it work because I couldn't bear to "lose" my initial investment.

The additional investment didn't save the business - it just increased my total losses. I would have been better off stopping after the first $3,000 loss and using that energy on a different opportunity.

> ▲ **Caution:** Past investments are costs, not assets. The money you've already spent is gone regardless of what you do next. Don't let loss aversion trap you in bad situations.

Combat loss aversion by reframing decisions in terms of future opportunities rather than past investments. Instead of "If I quit now, I'll lose everything I've invested," think "If I continue, what are the opportunity costs of not pursuing better alternatives?"

Set loss limits in advance, like stop-loss orders in stock trading. Decide before you start how much you're willing to lose on any venture, and stick to that limit regardless of how you feel when you reach it.

Remember that small losses early prevent large losses later. It's better to lose $500 testing an idea that doesn't work than to lose $5,000 trying to make a bad idea work.

Availability Heuristic: Overweighting Vivid Examples

Success stories are particularly vivid and memorable. When you hear about someone making $50,000 from a side hustle, that example sticks in your memory more than statistics about average outcomes. Your brain uses the ease of recalling this example as evidence that similar success is likely.

But vivid examples are often unrepresentative. The people with the most dramatic results (either positive or negative) are the most likely to share their stories. People with typical, moderate results don't create viral content or sell courses about their experiences.

Media coverage amplifies the availability heuristic by focusing on extreme examples. Articles about "22-year-old millionaire dropshippers" get more clicks than articles about "middle-aged consultant makes modest income from freelance work." The business media creates a distorted impression of typical outcomes by highlighting outliers.

I was influenced by the availability heuristic when I read about successful authors making six figures from self-published books. These stories were vivid and inspiring, making book publishing seem like a reliable path to significant income.

What I didn't consider was selection bias - I was only hearing from the most successful authors, not from the thousands who published books that sold poorly. The vivid success stories made me overestimate the probability of similar success.

> ★ **Pro Tip:** When evaluating opportunities, actively seek out information about typical outcomes, not just the most impressive success stories.

Combat the availability heuristic by looking for base rate information. What percentage of people who try this opportunity achieve various levels of success? What do median outcomes look like, not just the top performers?

Pay attention to time frames in success stories. "Made $100,000 in my first year" sounds impressive, but what happened in years two, three, and four? Some businesses have good first years followed by declining performance as market conditions change.

Look for comprehensive studies or surveys that provide representative data rather than relying on anecdotal examples. Academic research, industry reports, and platform-released statistics (when available) give more accurate pictures than individual success stories.

Cognitive Dissonance: Resolving Conflicting Information

In business contexts, cognitive dissonance often occurs when people have invested time or money in something that isn't working. Admitting the investment was a mistake creates psychological discomfort, so they change their beliefs about the investment's potential instead of changing their behavior.

"The course isn't working because I'm not implementing it correctly." "The strategy isn't working because the market is temporarily difficult." "I'm not making money yet because I haven't given it enough time." These explanations allow people to maintain their belief in the opportunity while avoiding the discomfort of admitting it was a poor choice.

Cognitive dissonance also occurs when people's actions conflict with their stated values. Someone who values financial security might pursue high-risk opportunities, creating psychological discomfort that gets resolved by convincing themselves the opportunities aren't risky.

I experienced cognitive dissonance when my affiliate marketing efforts weren't generating income. Instead of admitting the approach wasn't working for me, I convinced myself that I just needed to be more patient, try different products, or improve my marketing skills.

This allowed me to continue the approach without admitting that my initial judgment was wrong, but it prevented me from objectively evaluating whether my time would be better spent on different opportunities.

■ **Danger Zone:** When you find yourself making increasingly complex explanations for why something isn't working, you might be experiencing cognitive dissonance rather than objective analysis.

Reduce cognitive dissonance by separating your identity from your business decisions. A failed business experiment doesn't make you a failure - it makes you someone who tested an idea that didn't work out. Treating business decisions as experiments rather than reflections of your judgment makes it easier to change course when evidence does not support your hypotheses.

Create systems for objective evaluation that don't depend on your emotional state or psychological comfort. Track measurable outcomes and set criteria for success and failure that you decide in advance, when you're not emotionally invested in any particular outcome.

Seek outside perspectives from people who don't have emotional investments in your decisions. Friends, mentors, or advisors can often see situations more clearly than you can when you're experiencing cognitive dissonance.

The Antidotes: Systems for Better Decision-Making

Knowing about cognitive biases isn't enough. You need systems that help you make better decisions despite your brain's tendency toward predictable errors.

Create decision frameworks in advance. Before you start evaluating any opportunity, establish criteria for what would constitute success, what would constitute failure, and what information you would need to make an objective assessment. Write these criteria down and commit to following them.

Use outside view thinking. Instead of asking "Will this work for me?" ask "What percentage of people who try this approach succeed?" Base rate information is more reliable than inside view optimism about your specific situation.

Seek disconfirming evidence actively. For every positive piece of information about an opportunity, actively look for negative information. What are the failure rates? What are the hidden costs? What do critics say about this approach?

Set loss limits and stick to them. Decide in advance how much time and money you're willing to invest in any venture. When you reach these limits, stop regardless of how you feel about the sunk costs.

Track decisions and outcomes. Keep a record of business decisions you make, the reasoning behind them, and how they turn out. This helps you identify patterns in your thinking and improve your decision-making process.

▲ **Caution:** These systems only work if you use them consistently. It's easy to abandon good decision-making frameworks when you're excited about a new opportunity.

The goal isn't to eliminate all bias and emotion from business decisions - that's impossible and probably counterproductive. The goal is to recognize when bias is most likely to lead you astray and have systems in place to counteract the most dangerous thinking errors.

Your brain's shortcuts and biases served important functions in ancestral environments, and they still serve functions in modern life. But this space is full of people who profit from exploiting these mental patterns, so you need defenses against the most common forms of manipulation.

Good decision-making isn't about being perfectly rational. It's about being systematic in how you gather information, evaluate opportunities, and adapt when evidence changes. The mental traps are predictable, which means the antidotes are predictable too.

Recognize the patterns, use the systems, and make decisions based on evidence rather than emotions. Your financial future depends on it.

Here's what you now have that most people who try this don't have. You just read a map of the traps. The platforms designed to extract your time. The schemes that monetize desperation. The psychological patterns that keep smart, motivated people stuck in things that aren't working. Most people stumble into all of this blind and lose months figuring it out through trial and error and wasted money.

You're not going to do that. You know what the micro-income trap looks like before you've wasted a hundred hours on survey sites. You know why competing on price on Fiverr is a structural problem, not a tactics problem. You know why platform dependency is a business risk, not just an inconvenience. You know the seven mental patterns that trap people in failing strategies, and you have systems to counteract them. That knowledge is the difference between spending six months chasing the wrong things and spending that time building something real.

That's not discouragement. That's a head start. The next part of this book is about what works. It's shorter than what you just read, because figuring out what works is simpler than cataloguing what doesn't. But you needed the catalogue first. Now you have it.

If You Just Lost Your Job

Most of this book assumes you have a job and you're building an exit. If you just got laid off, that assumption is wrong and I want to address that directly before we go any further. And if you're reading this with nothing in your bank account (not a cushion, not a week's runway, nothing), I want to talk about that specifically, because most business books don't address it.

The methodology in this book still works for you. The principles are the same. What changes is the sequence, because when rent is due in six weeks, you can't afford to spend three months testing an idea that generates its first dollar in month four.

There's a difference between bridge work and building work. Bridge work is income you take to cover your immediate expenses while you figure out what you're building. It might be freelance gigs on platforms you'd eventually leave, temp work, contract assignments through your professional network, or consulting in the field you just left. It doesn't have to be the thing you build. Its only job is to buy you time.

Building work is what the rest of this book is about: developing income streams that compound over time, that you control, that don't depend on any single employer or platform. This work takes longer to generate income. It's worth doing, but it's not a substitute for this month's bills.

Run both in parallel. Use bridge work to stabilize your income while you run your first building experiments on the side. The experiments don't need to be large. Small, cheap tests that you can fit around whatever you're doing to pay the bills. When a building stream starts generating consistent income, you can reduce the bridge work. That's the same transition this book describes for people leaving jobs, just compressed and from a harder starting point.

Taking bridge work isn't a failure of the methodology. It's how you apply the methodology when your runway is short. The goal is the same: build income you control. The approach is the same too. You're just doing it with less margin for error, which means the testing discipline described in this book matters even more, not less.

I know someone (I'll call her a composite, because her story is more common than people admit) who lost her job on a Tuesday with no savings, no bank cushion, and rent due in three weeks. Not low savings. Zero. She didn't have the luxury of thinking about bridge work yet. She needed $40 that afternoon.

By that evening she was active on three delivery apps: Uber Eats, DoorDash, Grubhub. Not because delivery apps are a long-term strategy. Because delivery apps pay the same week and require nothing except a phone and a car. She also signed up for plasma donation. The clinic pays around $100 per session and allows donations on a set schedule, so she went as often as the rules allowed. She found two other same-day gig opportunities that paid on completion. None of this was a business. None of it was supposed to be. It was survival work: the category of income that exists to keep the electricity on while you figure out what comes next.

After a few weeks she had enough stability to think past the current one. She got a part-time job at a shop in a mall: predictable hours, predictable pay, a place to be every day. That's bridge work. Not what she wanted to do with her life. Not a business. Just a stable floor to stand on while she looked for something better. She kept the delivery work running alongside it during off hours.

A couple of months later she landed a database administrator role at higher pay than the job she'd lost. She kept the mall job for another month while the new income stabilized. Then she let it go. The delivery apps she wound down over time as they stopped being necessary.

That sequence (survival work, then bridge work, then building work, running in parallel and peeling off as each tier becomes unnecessary) is the actual playbook for zero-runway situations. It's not in most books because most books are written for people who have enough saved to plan. This one is trying not to make that assumption.

Survival work is: delivery apps, plasma donation, TaskRabbit, day labor, same-day gig platforms, anything that pays within 24–72 hours and requires no setup cost. It is not a long-term strategy. It doesn't need to be. Its only job is to buy you days. You do it until you have enough stability to think a week ahead instead of an afternoon ahead.

A note on the apparent contradiction: Part I of this book argues that delivery apps, platform gigs, and affiliate marketing are bad long-term strategies. That's still true. The distinction is what you're using them for. Using a delivery app to build a career is a trap. Using it to cover rent for six weeks while you figure out your next move is a rational decision about what the current 48 hours require. The tool isn't the problem. Mistaking a survival tool for a building tool is the problem. Survival work has one job: buy you enough time to think clearly. The moment it's doing that job, it's working correctly, and the moment you have enough stability to move to bridge or building work, you move.

Bridge work is: contract roles in your field, temp work, gig platforms that pay weekly, anything that generates reliable recurring income while you work on something longer-term. It buys you months, not days. It's what the rest of this section is about.

For people with professional skills, bridge work is usually faster to find than it feels like it should be. Your former employer or their competitors may need contract help in exactly the area you just left. Staffing agencies that specialize in your field, including IT, finance, HR, project management, legal, and healthcare, can often place you within days. LinkedIn is worth updating the same week you lose a job: former colleagues, managers, and clients are the fastest source of contract opportunities because they already know your work. You don't need to announce you're job hunting. You need to be visible and available. Most professional bridge work comes through people who already know you, not through cold applications.

Building work is what the rest of this book is about: income streams you own, that compound, that don't depend on a single employer or platform. It takes the longest to generate income. Don't start here if you have nothing in the bank. Start at survival work, move to bridge work as soon as you can, and begin building work in the margins once you have a floor under you.

None of this is failure. Showing up on a delivery app the same day you lost your job isn't giving up on your career. It's making a rational decision about what the next 48 hours require. The person in that story didn't abandon her professional life. She protected her ability to pursue it by refusing to let a cash emergency make her decisions for her.

Part II: What Works

What the Gig Economy Is (and Isn't)

When most people hear the term, they think of driving for Uber or delivering food for DoorDash. The media loves these stories because they're easy to understand and photograph. Worker drives car, worker gets paid, worker struggles to make ends meet. It's a neat narrative that fits into articles about the changing nature of work.

But that's not what this book is about. That version is just trading your time for money with extra steps and worse benefits. You're still working for someone else, following someone else's rules, and getting paid what someone else thinks you're worth. The only difference is that instead of one boss, you have an algorithm.

The version that can actually improve your life is about building multiple income streams that you control. It's about creating value on your own terms and capturing more of that value for yourself. It's about reducing your dependence on any single source of income, whether that's a traditional job or a gig platform.

Most advice on this gets it wrong. It focuses on tactics for squeezing more money out of existing platforms instead of strategies for building something sustainable. It treats symptoms instead of addressing the underlying problem, which is that depending on other people for your income is inherently risky.

The Real Definition vs. the Media Hype

The media defines the gig economy as short-term, flexible work arrangements facilitated by digital platforms.

Workers sign up for apps, complete tasks, and get paid per task. The platforms handle customer acquisition, payment processing, and dispute resolution. Workers provide labor and get a percentage of the transaction value.

This definition is technically accurate but practically useless. It describes the mechanics without explaining the economics. It focuses on the platforms without considering the workers' experience or outcomes.

Here's a better definition: the gig economy is the shift from employment-based income to project-based income. Instead of trading time for money on someone else's schedule, you're trading value for money on your own schedule. Instead of having one income source that controls your financial future, you have multiple income sources that you control.

The key word is "control." Traditional employment gives you very little control over your income. You work the hours they set, do the tasks they assign, and get paid what they decide you're worth. You can negotiate, but they have all the leverage because you need the job more than they need any individual employee.

The promise is more control. You choose which projects to take, when to work, how much to charge, and who to work with. You build skills and relationships that serve you instead of serving an employer. You create value that compounds instead of trading time for money that disappears as soon as you stop working.

Most people who try it don't get this control. They just replace one boss with many bosses, or worse, replace a human boss with an algorithmic boss that's even less reasonable and predictable.

The platforms market themselves as giving workers freedom and flexibility, but the reality is different. Uber drivers can't set their own rates. DoorDash drivers can't choose their delivery routes. TaskRabbit workers can't build direct relationships with their customers. The platforms maintain control while pushing the risks and costs onto the workers.

This isn't the gig economy - it's digital sharecropping. You're working someone else's land (platform) with someone else's tools (app) under someone else's rules (algorithm) and giving them the majority of the value you create. You get some money, but they get the customer relationship, the data, and the long-term value.

Real independent work is different. You control the relationship with your customers. You set your own prices. You build assets that appreciate. You capture more of the value you create instead of handing it over to a platform.

Traditional Gig Work vs. Online Income Streams

Traditional gig work - driving, delivering, cleaning, assembling furniture - is just hourly labor with extra steps. You're still trading time for money, but now you're also responsible for your own taxes, insurance, vehicle maintenance, and finding customers. You've taken on all the responsibilities of being a business owner without getting any of the benefits.

The math rarely works in your favor. Uber drivers gross about $15-20 per hour in most cities, but that's before expenses. After accounting for gas, maintenance, depreciation, and insurance, most drivers net closer to $10-12 per hour. Factor in the time spent driving to pickups and waiting between rides, and many drivers are making less than minimum wage.

The platforms know this, but they don't care. Their business model depends on having more drivers than rides, so there's always someone available when a customer opens the app. Driver oversupply keeps prices low and ensures fast pickup times, which is good for customers and platform profits but bad for driver earnings.

> ▲ **Caution:** Any platform that needs "more supply than demand" to function properly is designed to keep you poor.

The platforms also externalize most of their costs onto drivers. Drivers provide the vehicles, pay for gas and maintenance, handle customer service issues, and absorb the risk of accidents or difficult customers. The platforms provide the app and take 35-40% or more of every transaction for "facilitating" the connection.

This is why traditional gig work is a dead end. You're not building anything that compounds. You're not developing skills that become more valuable. You're not creating relationships that lead to better opportunities. You're just converting your time and vehicle equity into cash, and you're doing it inefficiently.

Online income streams are different. Instead of trading time for money, you're creating value that can be sold repeatedly. Instead of working in someone else's system, you're building your own system. Instead of competing on price and availability, you're competing on expertise and results.

When I write a book, I invest 50-100 hours of work upfront, but that book can generate income for years. Each sale doesn't require additional time from me - Amazon handles the printing, shipping, and customer service. The book is an asset that works while I sleep.

When I take on a ghostwriting client, I'm not just completing a task - I'm building a relationship that often leads to ongoing work. Clients refer me to their colleagues. The expertise I develop working with one client makes me more valuable to future clients. Each project builds on the previous ones.

That's what this actually looks like. You create value once and get paid for it multiple times. You build skills and relationships that appreciate. You develop expertise that commands higher rates. You create systems that scale beyond your personal time investment.

Why "Passive Income" is Mostly Bullshit

The phrase "passive income" has been ruined by internet marketers who use it to sell fantasies to desperate people. They promise income that requires no work, no maintenance, and no ongoing effort. Just set it up once and watch the money roll in forever.

This is bullshit. There's no such thing as truly passive income that doesn't require initial effort, ongoing maintenance, or significant upfront investment. Even the most "passive" income streams require work to create and work to maintain.

Real estate rental income isn't passive - you have to find properties, manage tenants, handle maintenance issues, and deal with vacancies. Dividend income isn't passive - you have to research companies, monitor your investments, and make decisions about when to buy and sell. Book royalties aren't passive - you have to write the books, market them, and keep them updated.

The people selling "passive income" courses are usually making their money from selling courses, not from the passive income streams they're teaching. Their real business model is convincing people that passive income is easy, then selling them information about how to create it.

But dismissing the concept entirely is a mistake too. There are income streams that require less ongoing time investment than traditional employment. There are ways to create value once and get paid for it repeatedly. There are systems that can generate money while you're sleeping, traveling, or working on other projects.

The key is understanding that these income streams aren't passive - they're leveraged. They allow you to create more value than you could by trading time for money directly. But they still require work to create and work to maintain.

My book publishing income is leveraged, not passive. I spend weeks writing each book, hours designing covers and formatting files, and ongoing time marketing and promoting. But once a book is published, it can generate sales for years without requiring additional writing time. Each sale doesn't demand new work from me.

My ghostwriting business has leveraged elements too. The systems I've built for interviewing clients, researching topics, and delivering finished pieces allow me to handle more clients without proportionally increasing my time investment. The reputation I've built allows me to charge higher rates for the same type of work.

These aren't passive income streams - they're scalable income streams. They allow me to create more value with less time investment, but they still require ongoing effort and attention.

The Difference Between Gig Work and Building Businesses

Most people doing gig work aren't building businesses - they're just self-employed workers. They complete tasks for money but don't create assets, build systems, or develop competitive advantages that last beyond each individual transaction.

A Fiverr seller who writes product descriptions for $5 each is doing gig work. They complete a task, get paid, and start over with the next task. There's no accumulated value from previous work. No competitive advantage. No system that makes the tenth task easier than the first task.

A writer who builds a content marketing agency is building a business. They develop expertise in specific industries, build relationships with clients who provide ongoing work, create systems for delivering consistent results, and eventually hire other writers to handle overflow work. Each project builds on previous projects.

The difference is whether you're creating assets that appreciate or just completing transactions that pay once and disappear.

Gig work focuses on completing tasks efficiently. Business building focuses on creating systems that generate ongoing value. Gig work optimizes for short-term income. Business building optimizes for long-term wealth creation.

Most platform-based work is gig work disguised as business building. The platforms want you to think you're building a business because it makes you more invested in their success. But you're not building anything you own or control. You're just completing tasks through someone else's system.

> ★ **Pro Tip:** If someone else can suspend your "business" with the click of a button, you don't have a business - you have a job with extra steps.

Real business building means creating income streams that you control. You own the customer relationships. You set the prices. You decide which projects to take and which to decline. You build assets - skills, reputation, systems, relationships - that become more valuable.

When I decided to focus on ghostwriting, I wasn't just taking on more ghostwriting tasks. I was building a ghostwriting business. I developed specialized expertise in business communication. I created systems for interviewing executives and extracting their ideas. I built relationships with clients who provided ongoing work and referrals.

After three years, I wasn't just a better ghostwriter - I had built something that was worth more than the sum of my individual skills. I had a reputation, a system, a client base, and expertise that would be difficult for someone else to replicate quickly.

That's the difference between doing gig work and building a business. Gig work makes you money today. Business building makes you money today and creates assets that make you money tomorrow.

Platform Dependency vs. Owning Your Income Streams

The biggest risk is platform dependency. When your income depends on someone else's platform, you're building your business on rented land. The platform can change its rules, adjust its algorithm, or eliminate your account without warning, and there's nothing you can do about it.

I've watched this happen across every platform. Amazon sellers who built six-figure businesses see their accounts suspended over policy violations they didn't know existed. YouTube creators lose their income overnight when the algorithm stops promoting their videos. Uber drivers in some cities see their rates cut by 30% with no advance notice.

> ■ **Danger Zone:** Building your entire income around a single platform is like building your house on quicksand. It looks stable until it isn't.

The platforms have all the power because they control access to customers. You might have great products or services, but if customers can't find you on the platform, you don't have a business. And the platforms can make you invisible whenever they want.

This is why platform-based income isn't really your income - it's the platform's income that they share with you as long as it serves their interests. When your interests and their interests diverge, they'll choose their interests every time.

Real income streams reduce your dependence on any single platform. That means owning your customer relationships. It means having multiple ways for customers to find and hire you. It means building assets that aren't controlled by someone else's algorithm.

When I ghostwrite for clients, I don't find those clients through a platform. I find them through referrals, through my website, through networking, and through my reputation in specific industries. Amazon could ban me tomorrow and it wouldn't affect my ghostwriting income because Amazon isn't part of that business.

When I publish books, I do use Amazon's platform, but I'm not dependent on their algorithm for discovery. I have an email list of readers who buy my books regardless of whether Amazon promotes them. I have a website where people can find my work directly. I have relationships with other authors who recommend my books to their audiences.

This doesn't mean avoiding platforms entirely. Platforms can be useful for customer acquisition, payment processing, and logistics. But they should be tools you use, not foundations you build on. You should be able to survive and thrive even if your least favorite platform disappeared tomorrow.

Why Most Advice Focuses on the Wrong Things

Most advice focuses on tactics for optimizing your performance on existing platforms. How to get more Uber rides. How to rank higher on Fiverr. How to get better reviews on TaskRabbit. How to increase your acceptance rate on DoorDash.

This advice treats the symptoms while ignoring the disease. The problem isn't that you're not optimizing your platform performance well enough. The problem is that you're trying to build a sustainable income using platforms that aren't designed to create sustainable income for workers.

The platforms are optimized for their own success, not yours. They want to maximize transaction volume while minimizing costs. Worker income is a cost to be minimized, not a benefit to be maximized. Any advice that assumes the platforms want you to succeed is based on a false premise.

> ⚠ **Caution:** Advice that teaches you to "hack" platform algorithms is usually obsolete by the time you learn it.

Even worse, most of this advice focuses on tactics that become obsolete quickly. The strategies for gaming Uber's algorithm in 2020 don't work today because the algorithm has changed. The techniques for ranking high on Fiverr last year don't work this year because the platform updated its search system.

You end up constantly chasing the latest tactics instead of building something sustainable. You become an expert at manipulating systems that can change overnight, instead of becoming an expert at creating value that people want to pay for.

The advice in this book is different. Instead of teaching you how to optimize your performance on someone else's platform, it teaches you how to build your own income streams. Instead of showing you how to compete more effectively for low-paying gigs, it shows you how to create high-value services that clients are eager to pay for.

Instead of helping you become a better digital sharecropper, it helps you become a digital landowner.

What We're Building: Multiple Income Streams That Scale

The goal isn't to replace your job with a single income stream. The goal is to build multiple income streams that collectively provide more security, flexibility, and earning potential than traditional employment.

Each income stream should have different characteristics:

Some should provide steady, predictable income that covers your basic expenses. These are your foundation streams - they might not be exciting, but they're reliable.

Some should provide high-earning potential that allows you to increase your income quickly when opportunities arise. These are your opportunity streams - they might be inconsistent, but they can be very profitable.

Some should provide passive or leveraged income that continues generating money even when you're not working. These are your scale streams - they might take time to build, but they can provide long-term wealth creation.

The specific mix depends on your skills, interests, risk tolerance, and financial situation. Someone with high expenses and low savings needs more foundation streams. Someone with financial cushion and high risk tolerance can focus more on opportunity and scale streams.

> ★ **Pro Tip:** Your income portfolio should be like a three-legged stool: stable (foundation), profitable (opportunity), and scalable (leveraged). Remove any leg and the whole thing falls over.

But the principle is the same: diversify your income sources so you're not dependent on any single stream, and structure each stream to provide maximum value with minimum ongoing time investment.

My current income portfolio includes:

Foundation stream: Long-term ghostwriting clients who provide predictable monthly income.

Opportunity stream: One-off ghostwriting projects that pay well but aren't recurring.

Scale stream: Book royalties that generate ongoing income from past work.

Each stream serves a different purpose and has different risk characteristics. If ghostwriting demand drops, book sales usually stay steady. If book sales drop, I can take on more one-off projects. If both drop, my long-term clients provide a baseline income while I figure out what's changed in the market.

This isn't just about financial security - it's about freedom. When you have multiple income streams, you can afford to be selective about which opportunities you pursue. You can turn down low-paying work because you're not desperate for any source of income. You can experiment with new ideas because you're not risking your entire livelihood.

You can take time off without losing income from your leveraged streams. You can travel without being tied to a specific location. You can focus on the work you enjoy most instead of just the work that pays the bills.

That's what this should be about: creating more freedom and control over your working life. Not trading one form of employment for a worse form of employment, but building something better than employment entirely.

The next chapters will show you how to build these income streams systematically. How to find opportunities that others miss. How to test ideas without risking significant time or money. How to scale what works and abandon what doesn't.

But first, you need to understand what you're trying to build. You're not trying to become a better gig worker. You're trying to become a business owner who happens to work online.

There's a big difference, and it changes everything about how you approach the work.

Everyone selling courses about freelancing focuses on the advantages. Work from anywhere! Be your own boss! Set your own schedule! Make unlimited income! They paint a picture of freedom and flexibility that sounds amazing to anyone stuck in a cubicle.

What they don't tell you about are the disadvantages. The feast or famine income cycles. The constant stress of finding new clients. The loneliness of working by yourself. The complexity of handling your own taxes, insurance, and business expenses. The psychological toll of never knowing how much money you'll make next month.

I'm not trying to scare you away from freelancing. I've been doing it for years and it's improved my life significantly. But you need to understand what you're signing up for. The fantasy version sold in courses and YouTube videos isn't reality. Reality is messier, harder, and more stressful than the marketing suggests.

It's also more rewarding, more flexible, and more financially lucrative than traditional employment - if you can handle the downsides. The key is going in with realistic expectations instead of fantasies that lead to disappointment and failure.

The Advantages That Are Real

Let's start with the good news. The advantages of freelancing and gig economy work are real - they're just not as simple or immediate as the marketers make them sound.

Income potential is genuinely higher. When you work for someone else, you get paid a fraction of the value you create. The company captures most of that value as profit. When you work for yourself, you capture more of the value you create. A ghostwriter working for a content agency might get paid $50 for an article that the agency sells to the client for $200. The same ghostwriter working directly with clients can charge $150-200 for the same article.

But this advantage only kicks in once you've figured out how to find clients, deliver quality work, and charge appropriate rates. In the beginning, you might make less than you would at a traditional job because you're still learning the business side of freelancing.

Flexibility is real, but it's not what you think. You can work from anywhere with an internet connection. You can set your own schedule. You can take time off without asking permission. You can structure your work around your life instead of structuring your life around your work.

> ★ **Pro Tip:** Flexibility doesn't mean working less - it means working when and where you're most productive.

But flexibility comes with responsibility. You have to be disciplined enough to work when you don't feel like it. You have to be organized enough to meet deadlines without a boss breathing down your neck. You have to be motivated enough to keep working when there's no immediate payoff.

You build transferable skills and assets. When you work for a company, you build skills that serve that company's needs. When you freelance, you build skills that serve your needs. You learn how to find customers, how to sell your services, how to deliver results, how to manage cash flow. These skills transfer to any business you might start in the future.

You also build assets that appreciate. Your reputation, your portfolio, your client relationships, your expertise - these things become more valuable as you gain experience. A traditional employee's main asset is their resume. A successful freelancer's assets include their reputation, their network, and their proven ability to generate income independently.

You have more control over your financial future. In traditional employment, your income is capped by salary bands, promotion schedules, and company policies. Your raises depend on your boss's mood and the company's budget. Your job security depends on factors completely outside your control.

When you freelance, your income depends on your ability to create value for clients. There's no artificial cap on what you can earn. There's no waiting for permission to increase your rates. There's no corporate restructuring that can eliminate your position overnight.

But this control comes with responsibility. You're responsible for finding clients, delivering results, managing your finances, and planning for the future. You can't blame your boss or your company when things go wrong.

The Disadvantages Nobody Talks About Until It's Too Late

Now for the bad news. The disadvantages of freelancing are real and significant. They're not deal-breakers for everyone, but they're serious enough that you need to understand them before you make the jump.

You have to be good at business, not just your skill. Being a great writer doesn't automatically make you a great freelance writer. Being a talented designer doesn't automatically make you a successful design consultant. You have to learn how to find clients, how to price your services, how to negotiate contracts, how to collect payments, how to handle difficult customers.

Many skilled professionals fail at freelancing not because they lack technical ability, but because they lack business skills. They can do the work, but they can't sell the work or manage the business side of freelancing.

> ■ **Danger Zone:** If you hate sales, marketing, and dealing with difficult people, freelancing will be miserable no matter how good you are at your core skill.

You're always working, even when you're not working. When you have a traditional job, you can leave work at the office. When you're a freelancer, work follows you everywhere. You're thinking about client projects during dinner. You're checking email on weekends. You're worried about cash flow when you're trying to fall asleep.

Even when you're not working on client projects, you're working on your business. You're marketing your services, following up with prospects, updating your portfolio, managing your finances, or planning your next move. The mental load never really stops.

You handle all the administrative burden. In traditional employment, someone else handles payroll, taxes, insurance, legal compliance, and benefits administration. When you're a freelancer, you handle all of this yourself or pay someone else to handle it for you.

You have to track your expenses, save for taxes, find your own health insurance, set up retirement accounts, and make sure you're complying with local business regulations. This administrative work is time-consuming, boring, and doesn't directly generate income.

You're responsible for your own professional development. Companies invest in employee training because they want their workers to be more productive. When you're a freelancer, you have to invest in your own training. You have to stay current with industry trends, learn new skills, and upgrade your knowledge - all on your own time and your own dime.

This is both a disadvantage and an advantage. You get to choose what skills to develop instead of being forced to learn whatever your employer thinks is important. But you also have to be disciplined enough to invest time and money in learning when you could be spending that time and money on other things.

Loneliness and isolation are real problems. Most freelancers work alone. You don't have coworkers to chat with, collaborate with, or complain to. You don't have office social events or water cooler conversations. You spend most of your day by yourself, interacting with clients through email and video calls.

> ▲ **Caution:** If you're someone who gets energy from being around other people, the isolation of freelancing might be harder than you expect.

Some people thrive in this environment. Others find it depressing and isolating. The lack of social interaction can affect your mental health, your motivation, and your professional development. You miss out on the informal learning that happens when you work closely with other people.

The Feast or Famine Problem

This is the biggest challenge that freelancers face, and it's the one that course sellers never mention because it makes freelancing sound less appealing.

Feast or famine means your income and workload swing between extremes. Either you have more work than you can handle, or you have no work at all. Either you're making great money and working 60-hour weeks, or you're making no money and desperately looking for clients.

This happens because of the pipeline problem. When you're busy with client work, you don't have time to market your services or pursue new opportunities. When you finish a big project, you suddenly have free time but no immediate income. You have to start the client acquisition process from scratch, which can take weeks or months to generate new revenue.

> ★ **Pro Tip:** The feast or famine cycle is why successful freelancers spend at least 20% of their time on marketing, even when they're busy with client work.

I learned this the hard way during my first year of ghostwriting. I landed a three-month project that paid well and kept me busy full-time. I was so focused on delivering great work that I stopped networking, stopped following up with prospects, and stopped marketing my services. When the project ended, I had no pipeline of new work. It took six weeks to find my next client, during which I made no money.

The psychological impact is worse than the financial impact. During feast periods, you feel successful and confident. You're making good money, clients love your work, and everything seems to be going well. During famine periods, you question everything. You wonder if you're cut out for freelancing. You consider going back to traditional employment. You stress about money and worry about the future.

Even successful freelancers with years of experience struggle with feast or famine cycles. The cycles get smaller and shorter as you get better at managing your pipeline, but they never completely disappear. There will always be months when you make less money than you expected and months when you make more money than you can handle.

The key is learning to manage the cycles instead of being victimized by them. You save money during feast periods to cover expenses during famine periods. You use famine periods to work on marketing, professional development, and business improvement. You build relationships and create systems that make the feast periods more predictable and the famine periods shorter.

But you can't eliminate the cycles entirely. Anyone who tells you they have "consistent monthly income" as a freelancer is either lying or has built something that's not really freelancing anymore (like a subscription-based consulting business or a productized service).

The Hidden Costs of Being Your Own Boss

When you work for someone else, many of your work-related expenses are covered by your employer. Your computer, your software, your office space, your internet connection, your phone - these costs are either provided by the company or tax-deductible as business expenses.

When you're a freelancer, you pay for everything yourself. You need a reliable computer, professional software, high-speed internet, a dedicated workspace, and probably a business phone line. You need to maintain and upgrade this equipment regularly. You need to have backup plans when technology fails.

You also need professional services that employees don't think about. You might need an accountant to handle your taxes, a lawyer to review contracts, a bookkeeper to manage your finances, and an insurance agent to find appropriate coverage. These services cost money and take time to manage.

★ **Pro Tip:** Budget at least 20-30% more for expenses than you think you'll need. There are always costs you don't anticipate.

The biggest hidden cost is time. You spend time on activities that don't directly generate income: marketing your services, following up with prospects, managing your finances, handling administrative tasks, learning new skills. This time is necessary for your business, but it reduces the number of billable hours you can work.

You also bear all the financial risks. If a client doesn't pay on time (or at all), you still have to cover your expenses. If you get sick and can't work, you don't earn money. If you take a vacation, you don't earn money unless you've built passive income streams.

The financial volatility requires different money management skills than traditional employment. You need larger emergency funds because your income is less predictable. You need to save for taxes because no one is withholding them from your pay. You need to plan for irregular income and irregular expenses.

The Benefits You Give Up

When you leave traditional employment, you don't just lose a salary - you lose a benefits package that's often worth 20-40% of your total compensation. Health insurance, retirement contributions, paid time off, disability insurance, life insurance - all of this disappears when you become a freelancer.

Health insurance is the biggest shock. What costs your employer $800/month might cost you $1,200/month for worse coverage with higher deductibles. That family plan that was "free" through your job? You're looking at $2,000-3,000/month to replace it independently.

Retirement benefits vanish too. No more employer 401k matching. No pension plan. No automatic payroll deductions that forced you to save. You have to set up your own retirement accounts, make your own contributions, and manage your own investments. Most freelancers are terrible at this because the money they should be saving for retirement gets eaten up by current expenses.

> ★ **Pro Tip:** When calculating whether freelancing pays better than your job, factor in the full cost of replacing your benefits package. You might need to charge 40-50% more than your salary just to break even.

Paid time off doesn't exist when you're freelancing. Sick days, vacation days, personal days - if you're not working, you're not earning. Take a two-week vacation and you lose two weeks of income. Get the flu and you lose a week of income while still having to cover your business expenses.

Disability insurance, life insurance, professional liability insurance - you need to buy all of this yourself. Workers' compensation doesn't exist for freelancers. If you get injured and can't work, there's no safety net except what you've built for yourself.

> ■ **Danger Zone:** Getting seriously sick or injured as a freelancer can bankrupt you in ways that employees with benefits never worry about.

The psychological impact is as significant as the financial impact. Knowing that getting sick or injured could wipe out your savings creates a constant low-level stress that employees don't experience. You can't just focus on your work - you're always thinking about what happens if you can't work.

The Psychological Challenges of Irregular Income

The mental and emotional challenges of irregular income are often harder to handle than the financial challenges. When your income varies dramatically from month to month, it affects how you think about money, how you plan for the future, and how you feel about your professional abilities.

During high-income months, you feel successful and confident. You're tempted to increase your spending, take on new financial commitments, or reward yourself for your success. During low-income months, you feel anxious and uncertain. You question your abilities, worry about your future, and regret any money you spent during the good times.

This emotional roller coaster is exhausting. You're constantly adjusting your financial expectations and your lifestyle based on recent income. You can't settle into a comfortable routine because your income never settles into a comfortable pattern.

> ■ **Danger Zone:** The psychological stress of irregular income can lead to poor financial decisions, like overspending during good months or taking on bad clients during slow months.

The uncertainty affects your relationships too. It's hard to make long-term plans when you don't know how much money you'll be making six months from now. It's stressful to split expenses with a partner when your income is unpredictable. It's difficult to explain to family and friends why you can afford something one month but not the next month.

You also miss the psychological comfort of routine that comes with traditional employment. There's something reassuring about knowing exactly how much money will hit your bank account every two weeks. There's comfort in having a predictable schedule, predictable responsibilities, and predictable income.

Freelancing replaces that comfort with uncertainty and responsibility. Some people thrive in this environment because they prefer control over comfort. Others find it too stressful and eventually return to traditional employment.

When Freelancing Makes Sense and When It Doesn't

Freelancing isn't right for everyone. It's not objectively better or worse than traditional employment - it's different, with different advantages and disadvantages that appeal to different personality types and life situations.

Freelancing makes sense if you value control over security. You'd prefer having multiple income sources that you control than one income source that someone else controls. You're comfortable with uncertainty. You can handle irregular income, changing client demands, and constantly evolving business conditions without losing sleep.

You enjoy business challenges. You find sales, marketing, and client management interesting instead of annoying. You like solving problems and building systems. You have strong self-discipline. You can work productively without supervision, meet deadlines without external pressure, and stay motivated during slow periods.

You're good at your core skill AND interested in learning business skills. You're willing to spend time on marketing, sales, and administration instead of just focusing on your technical abilities. You have financial reserves or low expenses. You can survive several months without income while you build your client base, or your living expenses are low enough that irregular income doesn't create serious hardship.

> ▲ **Caution:** Don't let anyone convince you that freelancing is objectively better than traditional employment. The best choice depends on your personality, your situation, and your priorities.

Freelancing doesn't make sense if you prioritize stability over control. You prefer predictable income and benefits over the potential for higher earnings and flexibility. You get overwhelmed by uncertainty. Irregular income, changing client demands, and business responsibilities create too much stress for you to be productive.

You hate sales and marketing. You just want to focus on your technical skills without dealing with client acquisition, contract negotiation, or business development. You need external structure and motivation. You work better when someone else sets your schedule, assigns your tasks, and holds you accountable for results.

You want to separate work from life. You prefer leaving work at the office instead of having business responsibilities follow you everywhere. If possible, you need financial cushion, some runway before you're dependent on what you're building. Otherwise, income from freelancing may take longer to arrive than your expenses can wait.

But runway is information, not a verdict. Knowing you have two months of savings doesn't mean you shouldn't start. It means you sequence differently. You may need bridge income while you run your first experiments. That's a constraint to plan around, not a reason to wait for better circumstances that may not arrive.

How to Know If You're Cut Out for This Lifestyle

The best way to know if freelancing is right for you is to try it while you still have the safety net of traditional employment. Take on small freelance projects during evenings and weekends. See how you handle the uncertainty, the client management, and the business responsibilities.

Pay attention to how you feel during the process. Do you get energized by finding new clients and solving business problems, or do you find it draining and stressful? Do you enjoy the variety and flexibility, or do you miss the structure and predictability of your day job?

Track your time and calculate your effective hourly rate. Include time spent on marketing, administration, and business development, not just billable client work. See if you're making more money per hour than you would in traditional employment.

Notice how you handle rejection and criticism. Clients will reject your proposals, complain about your work, and sometimes refuse to pay your bills. Freelancing requires a thick skin and the ability to separate your professional services from your personal worth.

★ **Pro Tip:** If you can't handle criticism of your work without taking it personally, freelancing will be emotionally brutal.

Test your financial discipline during the experiment. When you get paid for a freelance project, can you save part of that money for taxes and business expenses, or do you immediately spend it on something fun? Can you live on irregular income without constantly worrying about money?

Most importantly, pay attention to whether you enjoy the work itself more or less when you're doing it as a business instead of as a hobby or side project. Some people love their skill until they have to sell it to demanding clients under tight deadlines. Others find that the business context makes their work more interesting and meaningful.

Setting Realistic Expectations vs. the Fantasy

The fantasy version is seductive. Work from a beach in Thailand! Make six figures working part-time! Be your own boss and never answer to anyone again! Travel the world while building passive income streams!

The reality is messier. You'll work more hours than you expect, at least in the beginning. You'll make less money than you hope, at least until you figure out the business side. You'll deal with difficult clients, cash flow problems, and the constant stress of finding new work.

You'll also discover advantages that the marketers don't mention. You'll develop skills and confidence that serve you in every area of life. You'll build relationships with interesting people who become friends, mentors, and collaborators. You'll create something that's genuinely yours instead of building someone else's dream.

> ■ **Danger Zone:** Expect freelancing to be harder than traditional employment for at least the first year. Anyone who tells you it's easier is lying or selling something.

The key is going in with realistic expectations. Expect to struggle. Expect to make mistakes. Expect to earn less money and work more hours than you initially planned. Expect to question your decision multiple times during the first year.

But also expect to learn faster than you've ever learned before. Expect to develop capabilities you didn't know you had. Expect to have good months that make all the difficult months worthwhile. Expect to build something that's more valuable than just a paycheck.

Freelancing isn't for everyone, but it's not just for a special class of people either. Most of the skills you need can be learned. Most of the challenges can be overcome with time and experience. Most of the fears people have are based on worst-case scenarios that rarely happen.

The question isn't whether you're naturally suited for freelancing. The question is whether you're willing to learn what it takes and whether the advantages are worth the disadvantages for your specific situation.

If you're not sure, start small. Test the waters. See how it feels. You can always change your mind in either direction.

But don't base your decision on fantasy versions of either freelancing or traditional employment. Both have real advantages and real disadvantages. The best choice is the one that fits your personality, your goals, and your life circumstances.

Not the one that sounds the most appealing in a YouTube video.

Most people approach making money online like they're following a recipe. They find a successful person, copy their exact steps, and wonder why they get different results. It's like trying to recreate a master chef's signature dish by watching a five-minute YouTube video - you might get something edible, but it won't be the same.

The experimentation method is different. Instead of copying someone else's path, you create your own through systematic testing. You try small, cheap experiments to see what works for you, in your situation, with your skills and constraints. You scale what works and kill what doesn't. You build a portfolio of income streams that fit your life instead of trying to fit your life around someone else's business model.

This isn't about being original for the sake of being original. It's about recognizing that sustainable income comes from finding opportunities that others have missed, ignored, or dismissed. The best niches aren't the ones everyone is talking about - they're the ones nobody is talking about yet.

Find Your Own Niche, Don't Follow the Crowd

Every successful online business started with someone noticing an opportunity that others missed. The key word is "noticed," not "created." The opportunities were already there - they just needed someone to see them and act.

Most people look for opportunities in the wrong places. They look at what's already popular, what's already being taught in courses, what's already being done by thousands of other people. They're looking for validation that an opportunity exists by seeing other people succeed at it.

But here's the problem: by the time an opportunity is popular enough to be taught in courses and featured in YouTube videos, it's already past its prime. You're not getting in early - you're getting in late, after all the easy money has been extracted.

> ■ **Danger Zone:** If there's a course teaching "the exact system" for making money in a specific niche, that niche is already dead.

The real opportunities are hiding in plain sight. They're in the gaps between popular niches. They're in the problems that are too small for big companies to bother with but too profitable for small operators to ignore. They're in the intersections where your unique combination of skills, interests, and circumstances creates advantages that others can't replicate.

I found ghostwriting by accident. I was freelance writing for small businesses and kept getting asked to write content that the business owners would publish under their own names. White papers, blog posts, LinkedIn articles - stuff where they wanted to be seen as the expert but didn't have time to write it themselves.

Most writers saw this as a step down from bylined work. You don't get credit, you don't build a portfolio of published pieces with your name on them, you don't get the ego boost of seeing your writing attributed to you. The writing community looked down on ghostwriting as selling out.

But I realized that business owners would pay more for ghostwriting than for regular freelance work. They valued the time savings and the ability to maintain their personal brand. They didn't want a writer - they wanted a thinking partner who could capture their voice and ideas.

While other writers were competing for $50 blog post assignments, I was landing $500 ghostwriting projects. While they were building portfolios, I was building relationships with clients who came back month after month. While they were chasing bylines, I was chasing money.

> ★ **Pro Tip:** The best opportunities often look like "downgrades" to people who don't understand the economics.

Ghostwriting wasn't a plan. I stumbled into it by paying attention to what clients wanted instead of what I thought they should want. The opportunity was there all along - I just had to notice it and take it seriously.

Testing Opportunities with Minimal Cost and Risk

The biggest mistake people make when testing new opportunities is going all-in before they know if the opportunity works. They quit their jobs, invest their savings, and bet everything on an untested idea. When it doesn't work out, they're broke and demoralized.

Smart experimentation is about testing as cheaply as possible while still getting valid data. You want to prove or disprove your hypothesis without risking significant time or money. You want to fail fast and cheap if you're going to fail at all.

When I started testing book publishing, I didn't quit ghostwriting and write ten books. I wrote one short book on a topic I already knew well and published it on Amazon. Total time investment: about 20 hours spread over two weeks. Total money investment: $200 for a cover design.

The book made $47 in its first month. Not exactly retirement money, but it proved the concept worked. I could write books, people would buy them, and Amazon would handle the distribution and payment processing. The infrastructure was there - I just needed to figure out how to make it profitable.

I tested different topics, different lengths, different price points. Each test took minimal time and money because I was building on what I'd learned from previous tests. I wasn't starting from scratch each time - I was iterating.

Most tests failed. I wrote books that sold three copies. I tried topics that had no market demand. I experimented with pricing strategies that killed sales. But each failure taught me something, and the lessons accumulated into a system that worked.

> ▲ **Caution:** If you're not failing at least 70% of your experiments, you're not experimenting - you're just doing things you already know work.

The key to cheap testing is focusing on the biggest unknowns first. Don't spend time perfecting your website design until you know people want what you're selling. Don't invest in expensive tools until you know your basic concept works. Don't scale your marketing until you know your conversion rates.

Start with the riskiest assumption and test it as cheaply as possible. If that assumption is wrong, you've saved yourself months of wasted effort. If it's right, you can move on to testing the next biggest unknown.

How to Validate Ideas Before Major Investment

Validation isn't about asking people if they like your idea. People will lie to you to be polite. They'll say your idea is great even if they'd never buy what you're selling. They'll give you false encouragement that leads to real disappointment.

Validation is about getting people to take meaningful action that indicates real demand. It's about finding evidence that people will pay for what you're offering, not just evidence that they'll say nice things about it.

When I was considering expanding into technical writing, I didn't survey my network about whether they thought it was a good idea. I reached out to three software companies and offered to write a white paper for each of them at a discounted rate. Two of them said yes and paid me upfront.

That was validation. Not the fact that they said yes to a free consultation call, but the fact that they paid money for something I hadn't even created yet. Money is the ultimate form of validation because it represents real sacrifice and real commitment.

> ★ **Pro Tip:** People lie with their words but tell the truth with their wallets.

There are different levels of validation depending on what you're testing:

Interest validation is the weakest form. This is people signing up for your email list, downloading your free content, or engaging with your social media posts. It shows that people are curious about what you're doing, but it doesn't prove they'll pay for it.

Engagement validation is stronger. This is people spending significant time with your content, asking detailed questions, or sharing your work with others. It suggests deeper interest than casual browsing.

Commitment validation is the strongest form that doesn't involve money. This is people pre-ordering your product, signing up for a waiting list with their email address, or agreeing to be beta testers. They're making a small commitment that costs them something (even if it's just their email address).

Purchase validation is the gold standard. This is people paying money for what you're offering. It doesn't matter if it's $5 or $500 - the fact that they opened their wallet proves real demand exists.

Most people stop at interest validation. They get excited when people like their social media posts or sign up for their newsletter, and they interpret that as proof that their idea will work. But there's a huge gap between liking something and buying something.

I learned this the hard way when I was testing a course idea about freelance writing. I created a landing page describing the course and started collecting email addresses from people who wanted to be notified when it launched. I got 200 signups in two weeks and thought I had a hit.

When I launched the course, 12 people bought it. A 6% conversion rate from email signups to purchases. The other 188 people were just curious - they weren't ready to spend money to solve the problem I was addressing.

> ■ **Danger Zone:** Email signups are not customers. Social media followers are not customers. Only people who pay you money are customers.

Now I test purchase validation as early as possible. I'll create a simple sales page for a product that doesn't exist yet and see if people try to buy it. If they do, I build the product. If they don't, I save myself months of work.

This feels uncomfortable at first because you're essentially selling something you haven't created. But it's the only way to know if real demand exists before you invest significant time and money.

Scaling What Works, Killing What Doesn't

Most people are terrible at killing failed experiments. They get emotionally attached to ideas that aren't working and keep throwing time and money at them hoping they'll eventually succeed. They see giving up as failure instead of seeing it as smart resource allocation.

The sunk cost fallacy is dangerous when you're experimenting with income streams. Just because you've invested 50 hours in something doesn't mean you should invest 50 more hours if it's not working. The 50 hours are gone regardless - the question is whether the next 50 hours will be productive.

I spent three months trying to make money with online surveys before I admitted it was a waste of time. I kept telling myself I was getting better at finding the good surveys, that I was building up my ratings on the platforms, that I just needed to be more systematic about it. The truth was that surveys were fundamentally a bad use of my time, and no amount of optimization was going to change that.

When I finally calculated my hourly rate from survey work, it was $3.17. I was spending 10-15 hours a week making less than $50. A part-time job at McDonald's would have paid better and taught me more useful skills.

> ▲ **Caution:** Optimizing a fundamentally flawed strategy is like polishing a turd - you'll put in a lot of effort and still end up with shit.

But killing what doesn't work is only half the equation. The other half is scaling what does work, and most people are bad at this too. They find something that's working on a small scale and either try to scale it too quickly or don't scale it at all.

When I realized ghostwriting was profitable, I didn't immediately quit my other freelance work and go all-in on ghostwriting. I gradually shifted my focus. I started turning down regular freelance projects to make room for more ghostwriting clients. I raised my ghostwriting rates to see if demand was price-sensitive. I systemized my processes so I could handle more clients without working more hours.

The scaling process took about 18 months. I went from making $500 a month ghostwriting to making $12,000 a month, but it happened gradually as I learned how to find better clients, charge higher rates, and deliver more value.

Most people try to scale too fast. They find something that makes $500 a month and immediately try to turn it into $5,000 a month. They hire assistants before they understand the work well enough to train someone else. They invest in expensive tools before they know what tools they need. They expand into new markets before they've fully captured their current market.

> ★ **Pro Tip:** Double your income from existing streams before adding new streams. It's easier to do more of what's already working than to make something new work.

Smart scaling means doubling down on what's already working before you try to expand into new areas. If you're making $1,000 a month from one income stream, focus on getting that to $2,000 before you start testing new income streams. If you can get one client to pay you $500 a month, figure out how to get five clients to pay you $500 a month before you start looking for clients who'll pay $1,000.

The goal is to fully exploit an opportunity before you move on to the next one. Most opportunities have more potential than people realize, but that potential is only visible when you go deep instead of wide.

The Portfolio Approach: Multiple Income Streams for Stability

The traditional career advice is to specialize. Pick one thing, get really good at it, and build your entire professional identity around that expertise. This advice made sense when jobs were stable and careers were predictable, but it's dangerous in independent work.

When your income depends on platforms, algorithms, and market conditions that can change overnight, specialization is a risk you can't afford. You need multiple income streams that aren't correlated with each other, so when one stream dries up, you don't lose everything.

But most people approach multiple income streams wrong. They try to do five different things at 20% effort each, thinking that diversification means dividing their attention equally among many opportunities. This is a recipe for mediocrity in everything and mastery of nothing.

The portfolio approach is different. You focus most of your energy on one primary income stream until it's stable and profitable. Then you add a second income stream that complements the first. Then a third. Each new stream builds on the skills, relationships, and knowledge you've developed from previous streams.

My income portfolio developed organically over several years:

Primary stream: Ghostwriting for business executives. This required research skills, interviewing skills, and the ability to capture someone else's voice and ideas. It was relationship-dependent and service-based.

Secondary stream: Publishing my own books. This used the same writing skills but was product-based instead of service-based. It was less relationship-dependent but required marketing skills I didn't have for ghostwriting.

Tertiary stream: Freelance editing and consulting. This leveraged my writing expertise but required different types of client relationships. It was higher-hourly rate but lower-volume than ghostwriting.

Each stream used similar skills but had different risk profiles. Ghostwriting was high-touch and relationship-dependent, but it was also high-value and recurring. Book publishing was lower-touch and scalable, but it was also unpredictable and required ongoing marketing. Editing was somewhere in between.

When one stream had a bad month, the others usually stayed stable. When ghostwriting was slow, I could focus more energy on book marketing. When book sales were down, I could take on more editing projects. The streams balanced each other out.

> ★ **Pro Tip:** Good income streams should share skills but have different risk profiles. Think of it as diversification with synergy.

The key was that each stream informed and improved the others. The research I did for ghostwriting clients gave me ideas for books. The books established my expertise and attracted higher-quality ghostwriting clients. The editing work exposed me to different industries and writing styles that improved both my ghostwriting and my books.

This is different from having completely unrelated income streams. I've seen people try to combine affiliate marketing, dropshipping, and real estate investing because they heard you should diversify your income. But these activities require completely different skills, relationships, and resources. You can't apply knowledge from one to improve the others.

A good income portfolio has streams that are different enough to provide stability but similar enough to create synergies. The streams should share some common elements - skills, relationships, knowledge, or resources - so that success in one area contributes to success in the others.

Why Copying Others' Exact Methods Usually Fails

The biggest reason people fail at making money online is that they try to copy successful people's exact methods without understanding the context that made those methods work. They see the tactics but miss the strategy. They copy the surface-level actions but ignore the deeper principles.

When someone shares their success story, they're usually sharing the final version of their system - the polished, optimized result of months or years of experimentation. They're not sharing all the failed experiments, the dead ends, the pivots, and the lucky breaks that led to that final system.

You see a course creator making $50,000 a month selling courses about social media marketing. You think, "I'll create a course about social media marketing too." You copy their sales page structure, their pricing, their marketing tactics. Then you wonder why you sell three courses while they sell 300.

What you missed is that they spent two years building an audience before they launched their first course. They had 10,000 email subscribers and 50,000 social media followers who already trusted them. They had proven expertise from running successful social media campaigns for big clients. They had relationships with other influencers who promoted their course launch.

You had none of that context. You tried to copy their tactics without building the foundation that made those tactics effective. It's like trying to run the same play as a professional football team without having professional athletes, professional coaches, or professional training.

■ **Danger Zone:** Copying someone's final system without understanding their journey is like trying to build the roof before you've laid the foundation.

The same pattern happens across every niche. People see successful Amazon sellers and copy their product selection, pricing, and marketing without understanding how those sellers found their suppliers, built their brand recognition, or optimized their logistics. They see successful YouTubers and copy their video topics, thumbnail styles, and posting schedules without understanding how those creators developed their unique voice, built their audience, or navigated the platform's algorithm changes.

Context matters more than tactics. Your situation is different from theirs. Your skills are different. Your resources are different. Your constraints are different. Your market timing is different. Tactics that work for them might not work for you, and tactics that wouldn't work for them might be perfect for you.

This is why the experimentation method is more reliable than the copying method. Instead of trying to replicate someone else's success, you're trying to create your own success using methods that fit your specific situation.

When I started ghostwriting, I wasn't copying another ghostwriter's business model. I was responding to what my clients were asking for. I was building on my existing writing skills and my understanding of business communication. I was working within my constraints (limited startup capital, no business network, ADHD that made traditional employment difficult).

The system I built wouldn't work for everyone. It requires strong writing skills, the ability to interview executives and extract their ideas, comfort with not getting public credit for your work, and the patience to build long-term client relationships. Someone without those capabilities or inclinations should build a different system.

But the principles I used - identifying unmet client needs, testing small before scaling big, building on existing strengths, creating systems that work with your brain instead of against it - those principles are transferable. You can apply them to find opportunities that fit your situation instead of trying to force yourself into opportunities that fit someone else's situation.

> ▲ **Caution:** Learn principles, not tactics. Tactics become obsolete. Principles are timeless.

The goal isn't to avoid learning from successful people. The goal is to learn the right things. Learn their principles, not their tactics. Learn their thinking process, not their specific actions. Learn how they identify opportunities, how they test ideas, how they solve problems, how they make decisions.

Then apply that thinking to your own situation to create your own system. Your version won't look like theirs, but it will be better suited to your circumstances, which means it will be more likely to succeed.

The experimentation method gives you a framework for creating your own path instead of walking someone else's path. It's harder in the short term because you can't just follow a step-by-step guide. But it's more sustainable in the long term because you're building something that fits your life.

And when your system is working, you won't have to worry about someone else's system stopping working. You'll have learned how to build systems, not just how to operate them.

That's the difference between copying and creating. Copying makes you dependent on other people's thinking. Creating makes you independent.

Independence is what this is really about.

So here's the methodology, stripped down to what it actually is. Not a system you buy, not a blueprint you follow, but a repeatable thinking process you apply to your own situation.

Start with an honest inventory of what you already know and can do. Not just your job skills, but your hobbies, your life experience, the problems people ask you for help with. Most people skip this step because it feels too simple. It isn't. The gap between what you can do and what other people struggle with is where every opportunity lives.

Once you have a candidate opportunity, identify the riskiest assumption, not the hardest task, but the thing that has to be true for this to work at all. For ghostwriting, my riskiest assumption was that executives would actually pay more for unattributed work. Everything else was secondary. Test that assumption first, as cheaply as you can, before you build anything around it.

Before you run the test, write down what success looks like and what failure looks like. Do this before you start, not after you see the results. Your brain will rationalize almost any outcome if you let it evaluate without criteria. Set the criteria when you're thinking clearly, then hold yourself to them when the results come in.

Run the test and measure only what you defined. Not engagement, not encouraging signs, not "I think it's starting to work." The metric you set in advance. If it clears the bar, scale gradually, not all at once. If it doesn't, kill it and move on. The 50 hours you invested are gone either way. The question is what you do with the next 50.

Then repeat. The goal isn't one perfect income stream. It's a portfolio built through iterations, each one informed by the last. Most experiments will fail. That's not a sign you're doing it wrong. It's a sign you're doing it honestly. The ones that work will more than compensate for the ones that don't, and you'll understand your own strengths far better than any course could tell you.

Here's what the methodology looks like applied to something ordinary. Say you're decent at bookkeeping, not an accountant, but you manage your own finances carefully, you understand a P&L, and people have mentioned you seem unusually organized about money. That's the inventory step. Now you need a candidate: small business owners who handle their own books badly. That's not a guess. It's a known, chronic problem. The riskiest assumption isn't whether the problem exists. It's whether someone will pay a non-CPA to solve it.

Test that assumption first. Post in two local small business Facebook groups that you're offering a free 30-minute discovery call, just a conversation about their current setup and one specific recommendation. No sales pitch. Run three of those conversations in a week. Before you start, write down what success looks like: if at least one person says "I would actually pay for ongoing help with this," you have validation worth pursuing. If all three say "I have a system, thanks" or don't show up, you have useful data that cost you an evening.

If you get the signal, the next test is whether anyone will pay a small amount for a defined deliverable, say, reconciling one month of transactions for $75. Not a retainer, not a business plan. One concrete thing with a price on it. That tests purchase validation, not just interest. Set your success criteria before you run the test: one paying customer means the model works at small scale. Zero means either the price is wrong, the positioning is wrong, or the market is thinner than it looked.

Total investment so far: maybe eight hours and zero dollars. You haven't built a website, bought software, taken a course, or told anyone you're "starting a business." You've just run two cheap tests against two specific assumptions. If both clear, you scale. If either fails, you've learned something useful and lost nothing significant. That's the methodology, not as a theory, but as a sequence of actual steps you can take next week with whatever skill is on your list.

Here's what I don't want you to do after reading this chapter: try to copy exactly what I did or what the people in these case studies did. That's missing the point entirely.

These aren't instruction manuals. They're examples of how different people applied the experimentation method to find income streams that worked for their situations. The tactics they used might not work for you. The markets they entered might be saturated now. The skills they leveraged might not be skills you have.

But the principles they used are transferable. How they identified opportunities. How they tested ideas cheaply. How they scaled what worked and abandoned what didn't. How they built assets instead of just trading time for money. How they created systems that worked with their strengths instead of against them.

Your version won't look like theirs. Your opportunities will be different. Your constraints will be different. Your path will be different. But you can use the same thinking process to create something that fits your situation instead of trying to force yourself into someone else's mold.

Ghostwriting Case Study: How Skill Arbitrage Scales to $150,000/Year

Ghostwriting found me. I stumbled into it by paying attention to what clients were asking for instead of what I thought they should want.

I was doing freelance writing for small businesses: blog posts, web copy, newsletter content. Standard stuff that paid $25-75 per piece. The work was fine, but the market was crowded and the pay was mediocre. I was competing with thousands of other writers on price and turnaround time.

Then I noticed something. Several clients kept asking me to write content that they would publish under their names. LinkedIn articles for executives who didn't have time to write. White papers for consultants who wanted to establish thought leadership. Blog posts for business owners who needed content but didn't want to be seen as hiring outside writers.

Most writers I knew looked down on this work. No byline, no portfolio credit, no recognition. It felt like a step backward from "real" writing where your name appeared on the finished piece.

But I noticed these clients were willing to pay more for ghostwriting than for regular freelance work. A lot more. A blog post that might pay $50 with a byline would pay $200 as ghostwriting. A white paper that might pay $300 with attribution would pay $800 as ghostwriting.

> ★ **Pro Tip:** Sometimes the opportunities that look like downgrades to your peers are upgrades to your bank account.

The clients valued the time savings and the ability to maintain their personal brand. They didn't want a writer - they wanted a thinking partner who could capture their voice and ideas. They were willing to pay premium rates for someone who could interview them, extract their expertise, and turn it into polished content that sounded like them.

I started positioning myself as a ghostwriter instead of a freelance writer. I developed systems for interviewing executives, extracting their ideas, and capturing their voice. I learned about their industries so I could ask intelligent questions and understand their challenges.

The work was more complex than regular freelance writing, but it was also more interesting and much better paid. I was working with senior executives, learning about different industries, and solving communication problems instead of just filling content quotas.

Within 18 months, I was making $12,000/month from ghostwriting. Not because I was a better writer than other freelancers, but because I had found a niche where my skills were more valuable and the competition was less intense.

The key was skill arbitrage. I took skills that were common in the freelance writing market and applied them to a market where those skills were rare and valuable. Most executives can't write well, and most good writers don't understand business well enough to interview executives effectively.

> ■ **Danger Zone:** Don't try to become a ghostwriter because it worked for me. Try to find your own version of skill arbitrage based on your unique combination of abilities.

This isn't a blueprint for becoming a ghostwriter. It's an example of how to identify underserved niches where your existing skills are more valuable than they are in obvious markets.

From Hobby to Business: How Petra Turned Sewing into $60,000/Year

Petra Nakamura spent twelve years as an insurance administrator and sewed on nights and weekends to stay sane. She was good at it, better than she realized, because people who are surrounded by their own skill stop seeing it as unusual. Her machines were set up in the spare bedroom. Her fabric stash had quietly taken over a closet and half the garage. She had no plan to monetize any of it.

She posted a Facebook Marketplace listing almost as an afterthought: alterations and repairs, reasonable prices, pickup or drop-off. She expected nothing. The first week she got three inquiries. One of them asked if she could make a custom dress for a daughter's quinceañera because the ones in stores didn't fit right and the alterations quotes she'd gotten were nearly as expensive as a new dress. Petra quoted $180. The customer said yes before she finished the sentence.

The signal she was supposed to notice was buried in what customers kept asking for. Every time she posted an alteration job, someone in the comments asked about custom work. She ignored it for months because custom work felt complicated and she wasn't sure what to charge. Eventually she put up a listing for custom formal wear. She priced it too low, got booked out in two weeks, raised her prices, stayed booked. She raised them again. Still booked. This is how you find out where the ceiling actually is.

She left the insurance job eighteen months after the first Marketplace listing. At that point she had a two-month backlog, a waiting list she managed by email, and more referrals than she could take on. Her revenue that year was $47,000. The following year it crossed $60,000.

She never built an Etsy store. She never left her suburban market. The demand was already there. She just had to show up and follow where it pointed.

Public Speaking: From $500 to $20,000 Per Speech

Dmitri Kowalski was a mechanical engineer who'd spent eleven years working on industrial HVAC systems for commercial buildings. He was not a speaker. He had never wanted to be a speaker. He got volun-told into presenting at a regional facilities management conference because his company needed a body and he was the most junior person who knew the material. He prepared for three weeks, delivered the talk badly, and got more questions afterward than any other presenter on the program.

The questions were all the same type: how did you figure out it was a refrigerant specification problem and not a controls problem, how long did it take, what did it cost before you knew what you were looking for. He hadn't given a talk about HVAC systems. He'd given a talk about a $340,000 diagnostic mistake his company had made and how they eventually fixed it. Facilities managers who were responsible for buildings full of expensive equipment sat up when someone described a failure mode they hadn't considered and a resolution they could actually use.

He got asked to speak at two more conferences. He started charging a $500 honorarium because someone told him he should. Then $1,500. Then $3,500. The shift that changed his income wasn't the speaking fee. It was the conversation after a talk in Phoenix where a facilities director asked if he did in-house training. Dmitri said he'd never done it. The director said he'd pay $8,000 for a full-day session with his maintenance team. Dmitri said yes, built the session on the flight home, and delivered it six weeks later.

Corporate training is now the majority of his income. He charges $12,000 to $18,000 per day depending on group size and travel. He does eight to twelve engagements a year and turns down more than he takes. His delivery still isn't polished. Nobody has ever hired him for his delivery. They hire him because he can describe, in specific operational terms, what goes wrong and what it costs, and that knowledge is worth considerably more than a day of his time.

The mechanics of Dmitri's transition are worth unpacking because they apply to anyone moving from occasional speaker to paid engagement. Three things drove the shift, and none of them involved getting better at presenting.

First, he stopped pitching himself and started following inbound. Every paid engagement he has ever taken came from someone in the audience who approached him afterward. He has never cold-pitched a speaking engagement. The talk is the pitch, not for himself as a speaker, but for the problem he solves. Facilities managers who hear him describe a $340,000 diagnostic failure and its resolution immediately ask themselves whether their buildings have the same vulnerability. That question is what generates the follow-up conversation.

Second, he learned to price the outcome rather than the day. When a facilities director offers to pay someone $8,000 for a full-day training session, he is not paying for eight hours of Dmitri's time. He is paying to reduce the probability that his maintenance team makes a $340,000 mistake. Those are completely different purchases. A day rate is a cost. Failure prevention is an investment. Dmitri quotes based on what the problem costs the client: what a bad diagnostic, a missed failure mode, or an unplanned outage actually runs in a building his size. His rate is a fraction of that number. The client does the math and says yes.

That pattern, pricing based on what the problem costs rather than what the work takes, is the core principle for anyone selling technical expertise to clients who don't fully understand it. Don't ask what your time is worth. Ask what the problem costs. Then price yourself as a fraction of that. A client who doesn't understand your methodology will resist a day rate. A client who understands what they're preventing will rarely push back on the same number framed as risk reduction.

Third, he built a clear transition from speaking fee to training engagement. The conference talk establishes credibility and surfaces the right clients. The post-talk conversation identifies whether the problem is real and specific in their organization. The follow-up proposal narrows the training scope to exactly the failure modes that came up in that conversation. By the time he quotes a number, the client has already convinced themselves they need it. He is not selling a training day. He is confirming that yes, he can do the specific thing they just told him they need.

★ **Pro Tip:** If you do any kind of speaking, teaching, or public presenting, treat every session as a business development call for your consulting work, not as an end in itself. The fee for the talk is not the point. The conversations afterward are.

For anyone with deep technical expertise considering this path: the barrier is not getting polished. Dmitri's delivery is still uneven and he knows it. The barrier is identifying the failure mode that keeps your target audience awake at night and being able to describe it in operational terms they recognize. That's the whole job. Everything else follows.

When Necessity Removes the Option of Waiting

Rosa wasn't optimizing her career. She was disabled, which meant conventional employment wasn't a real option, and she needed income that she could control and do on her own terms. What she had was an industrial sewing setup: multiple machines, years of skill, and enough inventory that her house had become a supply room. She opened an Etsy store offering custom outfits and clothing repair. Two revenue streams from the same skill, zero startup cost because the equipment already existed. The business didn't come from a plan or a pivot. It came from looking honestly at what she had, what she could do, and what the actual constraints were. She's doing well. The point isn't the sewing. It's that the answer was already there once she stopped looking for options that weren't available to her.

These principles can be applied to almost any skill or situation. The tactics will be different, but the thinking process is the same.

How to Find Your Own Version Based on Your Skills

The goal isn't to become a ghostwriter, seamstress, speaker, or author. The goal is to find your own version of skill arbitrage based on your unique combination of abilities, interests, and circumstances.

Start by inventorying what you already know and can do. Don't just think about your job skills - think about your hobbies, your personal interests, your life experiences. Petra's sewing hobby became a business. Dmitri's reluctant conference speaking became a career.

The hardest part of the inventory step is that the most valuable skills are usually invisible to the person who has them. You've been doing something for years, so it feels ordinary. Work through these six categories and write down everything, even things that feel too obvious or too small.

What your job actually taught you. Not your job title, but what you actually know how to do because of the work. A project manager knows how to run meetings that don't waste time, write requirements that contractors can follow, and tell when a project is in trouble before it's officially in trouble. A nurse knows how to explain medical situations to frightened people. An accountant knows where small businesses bleed money without realizing it. None of that is on the resume. All of it is sellable.

What you've learned the hard way. Problems you've solved that cost you real money, time, or pain to figure out. Getting out of debt. Navigating a difficult divorce. Managing a chronic health condition. Starting over in a new city. The knowledge you earned through difficulty is often exactly what someone earlier in the same situation would pay for.

What people assume you can help with. Not what you offer, but what people ask you about. Friends, family, coworkers. When someone at a party finds out what you do and says "oh, you'd know about this," what's the this?

When colleagues forward you problems that aren't technically your job, what kind of problems are they?

What you know about an industry from the inside. If you've worked in healthcare, finance, construction, education, or any other sector for more than a few years, you understand how that world actually works, not how it looks from outside. That knowledge is valuable to people trying to enter that industry, market to it, or navigate it as a customer.

What you've built or made outside of work. Renovations. Restorations. Gardens. Software tools. Creative projects. Physical things. Skills you developed for their own sake often represent real competence that other people would pay for.

What you've taught yourself to solve a recurring problem. Self-taught bookkeeping to manage a small business. Home brewing that turned into understanding fermentation chemistry. Caring for an aging parent that turned into understanding the Medicare system. Necessity-driven learning is often deeper than formal training.

Once you have the list, mark anything where someone has already paid money for that skill or knowledge, even informally. A neighbor paid you to help with something. A friend referred you to someone who hired you. You got pulled into a consulting role that wasn't your job. That payment, even casual payment, is the signal that a market exists. Start with those candidates first.

Look for intersections between your skills and other people's problems. What do you know how to do that other people struggle with? What problems do you solve regularly that others find difficult or time-consuming?

Pay attention to what people ask you for help with. Friends, family, coworkers - what do they come to you for advice about? What do they assume you can help them with? These informal requests often point to skills that you take for granted but others value.

Consider your unique perspective and experience. What combination of skills, knowledge, and background do you have that's different from most people? Dmitri combined deep operational knowledge from eleven years of engineering work with the ability to explain technical failures to non-engineers. Petra combined sewing skills with understanding of local market needs.

> ■ **Danger Zone:** Don't try to force yourself into someone else's successful model. Find opportunities that fit your skills and circumstances.

Test small before you commit big. Petra started with Facebook Marketplace posts, not a full sewing business. Dmitri started with better conference presentations, not a speaking career. I started with one short book, not a publishing empire.

Look for markets where your skills are undervalued or underserved. The money isn't in competing with thousands of other people doing exactly the same thing. The money is in finding niches where your combination of skills is rare and valuable.

Once you have a list of candidates, the hard part isn't generating ideas. It's narrowing to the one worth testing first. Three questions help: First, have you already seen evidence that people pay for this, even informally? Not proof, just a signal. Second, can you run a meaningful test in under a week without significant money or infrastructure? If the test itself requires building a website, hiring someone, or taking a course first, the barrier is too high. Third, do you have enough genuine interest in the subject to work on it during slow periods when nothing is working yet? Skills you're competent at but indifferent to tend to stall when the initial enthusiasm wears off. The candidate that scores best on all three is the one to test first, not the most exciting one, not the highest potential one, just the one where the signal, the testability, and your own durability all point the same direction.

Creating Assets vs. Trading Time for Money

The difference between a job and a business is the difference between trading time for money and creating assets that generate money.

When you have a job, you trade your time for someone else's money. When you stop working, the money stops coming. Your income is directly tied to your hours worked.

When you build a business, you create assets that can generate money even when you're not working. Your reputation, your client relationships, your systems, your products - these things have value beyond the immediate work you do.

Petra didn't just do alterations for money. She built a reputation and a client base that referred new customers to her. She created systems for managing her workflow and pricing her services. She developed expertise in custom work that commanded higher rates.

Dmitri didn't just speak for fees. He built a reputation as an expert in technical areas. He developed content and case studies that he could reuse in different formats. He created relationships with companies that led to ongoing consulting work.

My books aren't just products that generate royalties. They're marketing tools that establish credibility and attract higher-paying clients. They're assets that work 24/7 to promote my expertise and generate leads.

★ **Pro Tip:** Always ask yourself: "Am I just trading time for money, or am I building something that becomes more valuable?"

The goal is to move from purely time-based income to asset-based income. You start by trading time for money because that's how you learn your market and build your skills. But you gradually create systems, relationships, and products that generate income beyond your direct time investment.

Geographic and Economic Arbitrage Opportunities

One advantage of online income streams is that you can live anywhere while serving customers anywhere. This creates opportunities for both geographic arbitrage (living somewhere cheap while earning money from somewhere expensive) and economic arbitrage (leveraging differences in local market conditions).

If you can do work remotely, you can live in a low-cost area while charging rates based on high-cost markets. A ghostwriter living in rural Iowa can charge New York City rates while paying Iowa living expenses. A consultant living in Austin can serve San Francisco clients without San Francisco overhead.

But geographic arbitrage isn't just about living somewhere cheap. It's also about finding underserved local markets where your skills are rare. Petra's sewing business worked partly because she was in a suburban area where good seamstresses were hard to find. Dmitri's speaking business worked partly because he was in a tech hub where companies regularly needed technical training.

Economic arbitrage means leveraging differences in what people can afford and what they're willing to pay. A service that's too expensive for small businesses might be affordable for enterprise clients. A product that's too cheap for luxury markets might be perfect for budget-conscious consumers.

> ▲ **Caution:** Don't assume that cheap locations automatically mean better opportunities. Sometimes expensive locations have more customers who can afford premium services.

The key is understanding that different markets have different dynamics. What works in one geographic or economic context might not work in another. But the principles of identifying underserved needs and providing valuable solutions work everywhere.

Your version of these opportunities will depend on where you are, what you can do, and who you can serve. But the examples in this chapter show that almost any skill can be turned into income if you apply the right thinking and find the right market.

Don't copy the tactics. Copy the thinking.

This world is full of predators. They're selling dreams to desperate people, promising easy money for minimal effort, and targeting anyone who's struggling financially or dissatisfied with their current situation.

These predators have gotten sophisticated. They don't look like the obvious scammers from 20 years ago with their broken English and Nigerian prince emails. Today's scammers have professional websites, polished sales videos, and testimonials from "successful" users. They've learned to speak the language of entrepreneurship and personal development to make their schemes sound legitimate.

The problem isn't just avoiding obvious scams. The problem is that many "legitimate" opportunities in this space are designed to extract value from you while giving you just enough hope to keep you engaged. They're not technically scams, but they're not genuine opportunities either.

You need to develop radar for bullshit. You need to understand the warning signs of unsustainable schemes. You need to know when to walk away from opportunities that aren't working. Most importantly, you need to structure your income streams so that when one fails (and they will fail), you don't lose everything.

Stay Away from Risky Schemes and the MLM Plague

Let's start with the obvious stuff: multi-level marketing schemes and get-rich-quick programs that promise unrealistic returns for minimal effort.

MLM schemes are insidious because they're technically legal and often marketed as entrepreneurship or small business ownership. They prey on people's desire for financial independence and wrap their predatory business model in the language of empowerment and community.

Here's how to spot an MLM: if success depends on recruiting other people instead of selling products to end customers, it's an MLM. If the real money comes from building a "downline" instead of from the product or service, it's an MLM. If they use terms like "network marketing," "direct sales," or "social selling," it's probably an MLM.

> ■ **Danger Zone:** If someone tries to recruit you by showing income screenshots from their upline instead of from selling products, run.

MLMs don't work for 99% of participants. The Federal Trade Commission's own data shows that most MLM participants lose money when you factor in their time and expenses. The people who make money are the ones who got in early and built large downlines before the market became saturated.

But MLMs are just the most obvious example of schemes that don't work. There are subtler versions that use the same psychology but avoid the legal definition of pyramid schemes.

"Business opportunities" that require upfront investment for training materials, starter kits, or exclusive territories are usually scams. Legitimate businesses don't charge you for the privilege of working for them. If someone wants money upfront before you can start earning, it's probably a scam.

"Guaranteed income" programs are always scams. No legitimate business can guarantee income levels because income depends on factors outside anyone's control: market demand, competition, economic conditions, your own effort and skill level. Anyone promising guaranteed returns is lying.

> ★ **Pro Tip:** Legitimate opportunities get more attractive the more you research them. Scams get less attractive the more you research them.

High-pressure sales tactics are another red flag. Legitimate opportunities don't disappear if you take time to think about them. If someone is pressuring you to "act now" or "take advantage of this limited-time offer," they're probably trying to prevent you from doing research or thinking clearly.

Red Flags That Scream "Scam" or "Unsustainable"

Beyond obvious MLMs and get-rich-quick schemes, there are subtler warning signs that an opportunity isn't what it appears to be.

Income claims without context. Screenshots of earnings that don't show time investment, expenses, or how long it took to reach those levels. A screenshot showing someone made $10,000 in a month is meaningless without knowing they spent $8,000 on ads, worked 80 hours a week, and it was their best month after six months of making nothing.

Success stories that are too good to be true. People who went from broke to millionaire in six months.

College students making $50,000 a month. Stay-at-home parents replacing their spouse's six-figure income working part-time. These stories are either completely fake or represent lottery-winner-level outliers that aren't representative of typical results.

Vague descriptions of what you'll be doing. "Digital marketing," "e-commerce," "online business," "social media monetization" - these terms don't tell you anything about the work involved. Legitimate opportunities can be described clearly.

Focus on lifestyle instead of work. Marketing that emphasizes traveling the world, working from the beach, or having unlimited free time while making great money. Real businesses require real work. If the marketing focuses more on the lifestyle than on the value you'll create for customers, it's probably targeting your fantasies instead of offering a genuine opportunity.

> ▲ **Caution:** Be suspicious of opportunities that seem too good to be true for your skill level or experience. Real opportunities usually require relevant skills or significant learning.

Testimonials without verification. Success stories from people who are only identified by first name and last initial. Video testimonials from people who could be actors. Screenshots of earnings that could be easily faked. Legitimate businesses can provide verifiable references and case studies.

Complex compensation structures. If you need a flowchart to understand how you'll get paid, it's probably designed to confuse you. Legitimate work has straightforward compensation: you provide value, you get paid a clear amount.

Emphasis on recruiting instead of customers. Even programs that aren't technically MLMs can have MLM-like characteristics. If the focus is on building a team or getting referrals instead of serving customers, the business model is probably unsustainable.

Required purchases from the company. "Business opportunities" that require you to buy products from the company you're supposedly working with. This is a classic sign that the real customers are the people trying to make money, not the end users of the product.

Real Scams, Real Patterns

The red flags in this chapter aren't hypothetical. The three scams described below are ones I encountered personally, documented in detail on my website with the full mechanics of how each one worked. They're worth reading before you start approaching clients, because knowing the pattern is what lets you spot it before you're inside it.

The content harvesting scam. A sophisticated operator used a legitimate real estate company as cover to solicit paid writing samples from hundreds of freelancers simultaneously. The budget looked real. The business was real. The project didn't exist. The samples were the product. Full details: thewritingking.com/ghostwriting-scam/

The overpayment scam. A scammer spent a month building a believable $90,000 ghostwriting relationship before revealing the mechanics: an overpayment that would require me to forward money to a third party. The payment was fake. The forwarded money would have been real. The tell was cybersecurity training, twenty-five years of it. Full details: <u>thewritingking.com/caribbean-scam/</u>

The three-scam playbook. A consolidated breakdown of the overpayment scam, the content harvesting scam, and the fake business scam, including the seven red flags that appear across all three and how to protect yourself from each. Worth bookmarking: <u>thewritingking.com/art-scam/</u>

How much verification to do depends on what's at stake. A small first engagement with a warm contact needs a phone call and basic online presence. A large project with someone you've never met warrants more. Scale your due diligence to the size of the risk.

Verifying a New Client Before You Start

For any engagement over a few hundred dollars with someone you don't already know, run through this sequence before you sign anything or do any work. The level of verification should match the size of the engagement.

Phone call first. Always. Before anything else, before a sample, before a proposal, before an SOW. Legitimate clients with real projects want to talk about them. A real person with a real need is eager to explain the project, ask questions about your process, and start building the relationship that will carry the work. A scammer avoids the call because conversation requires real-time improvisation they haven't prepared for. If a potential client refuses to get on a phone call and instead pushes straight to a sample, a contract, or payment, that refusal is your answer.

For mid-size or larger engagements, add a video call. Seeing a person's face on camera is a meaningfully higher bar than a voice call. It's harder to sustain a fabricated identity on video. You also read things that audio alone doesn't give you: hesitation, inconsistency, mismatches between what they're saying and how they're saying it. Ask them to turn the camera on. Legitimate clients don't find this strange.

Check LinkedIn before the call, not after. A professional with the credentials they claim will have a LinkedIn history that supports those claims: connections, employment history, posts, endorsements that accumulated over time rather than a profile created three weeks ago. Look for the gap between the entity and the individual: the business may be real and well-established while the person using it to contact freelancers has no professional footprint that connects to the project they're proposing. A "business consultant" with no LinkedIn presence, a "published author" with no books you can find, a "gallery director" whose gallery was created last month. These are gaps worth probing before you invest time or work.

For significant engagements, verify the business independently. Look up the company separately from whatever the client sent you. Don't use the links in their email. Search the company name, check state business registrations, look for reviews or mentions that didn't originate from the person trying to hire you. A real business has a footprint that exists independently of its own marketing. If the only evidence a business exists comes from materials the potential client provided, that's not verification.

Search their name plus the word "scam." It takes ten seconds and has saved people significant money. Scammers often run the same operation repeatedly against multiple freelancers in the same field. If someone has done this before, there is frequently a report somewhere.

The One Rule You Cannot Break: Never Forward Money

The overpayment scam has one essential mechanic: they send you more than they owe and ask you to send the difference somewhere else. The payment they sent is fraudulent: a fake check, a reversed wire, a payment that will bounce or be clawed back. The money you forwarded was real. You are out whatever you sent, plus whatever your bank charges for the fraudulent deposit, plus potentially held liable for the full original amount if your bank comes after you.

The stories change. The accounting department made an error. The extra amount is for materials you'll need to buy. The additional funds are for a consultant or project manager who handles the financial side. There's a currency exchange issue that requires routing through a US account. The framing is always plausible, always explained away with a business-sounding reason, always presented as a minor administrative inconvenience rather than the fraud it is.

The rule is simple and has no exceptions: you do not forward money to anyone for any reason in connection with a client engagement. Not a partial refund. Not an overpayment correction. Not a third-party consultant fee. Not a materials advance. If a client sends you more than the agreed amount and asks you to send any portion of it anywhere, the engagement is a scam. End the conversation. Do not send the money. Do not wait to see if the original payment clears, since fraudulent payments are designed to appear valid for days before they fail.

■ **Danger Zone:** A payment that has "posted" to your account is not the same as a payment that has cleared. Banks make funds available before checks and certain transfers are fully verified. A check can appear in your balance and still bounce five to ten business days later. If you forwarded money against a payment that hadn't fully cleared, you are liable for what you sent. Do not treat any payment as real until it has been in your account long enough to have fully cleared. Ask your bank what that window is for the payment type in question.

This rule applies regardless of how the client explains it, how established the relationship feels, how much you need the work, or how embarrassing it would be to have misread the situation. The embarrassment of walking away from a scam is nothing compared to the loss of forwarding real money against a fraudulent payment. If any client, new or established, asks you to forward money for any reason, the answer is no. Every time. Without exception.

Platform Dependency Risks and Diversification Strategies

Even legitimate opportunities carry risks if you become too dependent on someone else's platform. When your income depends on a single platform, algorithm, or company, you're building your business on rented land.

Platform dependency risk isn't just about the platform shutting down (though that happens). It's about the platform changing rules, adjusting algorithms, or modifying fee structures in ways that kill your profitability.

I've watched Amazon sellers lose their businesses overnight when Amazon decided their products violated new policies. I've seen YouTube creators go from six-figure incomes to nothing when the algorithm stopped promoting their content. I've watched Uber drivers see their effective hourly rates cut in half when the company changed pricing structures.

The platforms have all the power because they control access to customers. They can make you invisible with a single algorithm change. They can suspend your account based on customer complaints or automated systems. They can change their fee structure and there's nothing you can do about it.

> ■ **Danger Zone:** If losing access to one platform would eliminate more than 50% of your income, you're dangerously over-concentrated.

The solution isn't to avoid platforms entirely - they can be useful tools for customer acquisition and order fulfillment. The solution is to build your business so that you're not dependent on any single platform for the majority of your income.

Diversify your customer acquisition. Don't rely on one platform to find all your customers. If you sell on Amazon, also sell on your own website. If you find clients through LinkedIn, also build referral relationships and a personal network. If you get traffic from Google, also build an email list and social media following.

Own your customer relationships. Collect email addresses, phone numbers, and other contact information so you can reach customers directly. Build a database of clients who can hire you again regardless of whether any platform promotes your services.

Build multiple income streams on different platforms. If you're successful selling physical products on Amazon, don't expand by selling more products on Amazon. Expand by offering services on a different platform or creating digital products that don't depend on Amazon at all.

Create platform-independent assets. Your email list, your website, your reputation, your skills - these things have value regardless of what happens to any platform. Focus on building assets that you control instead of assets that exist only within someone else's system.

> ★ **Pro Tip:** The best platforms are the ones you can walk away from without losing your business. If you can't walk away, you don't have leverage.

This doesn't mean you should avoid all platform-dependent opportunities. Many successful businesses started by using platforms and gradually reduced their dependence. But you should always be working toward independence, not deeper dependence.

Building Multiple Streams Because You Never Know What Will Die

Income diversification isn't just about risk management - it's about recognizing that all opportunities have lifecycles. What works today might not work tomorrow. Markets change, platforms evolve, customer preferences shift, new competitors emerge.

The goal isn't to find one perfect income stream that will last forever. The goal is to build a portfolio of income streams that collectively provide stability even when individual streams fluctuate or disappear.

Think like a venture capitalist investing in startups. Most startups fail, so VCs invest in multiple companies expecting that one or two big successes will make up for several failures. You should approach income streams the same way - expect some to fail, but build enough of them that your overall portfolio succeeds.

Build streams with different risk profiles. Some should be stable and predictable (even if they don't pay much). Some should have high growth potential (even if they're risky). Some should be passive or leveraged (even if they take time to build). The mix should balance current income needs with long-term wealth building.

Create streams that aren't correlated. If one stream fails, the others shouldn't fail for the same reason. Don't build three different Amazon businesses - that's not diversification, that's concentration. Build streams that depend on different platforms, serve different markets, and use different skill sets.

My income portfolio illustrates this principle. Ghostwriting provides stable, recurring income but depends on my time and health. Book publishing provides leveraged income but depends on Amazon's platform and algorithm. Editing and consulting provide high-hourly income but are project-based and unpredictable.

When ghostwriting is slow, I can focus more on book marketing or take on editing projects. When Amazon changes its algorithm and book sales drop, my ghostwriting clients still need monthly content. When I'm too busy with client work to market books effectively, the passive income continues.

> ▲ **Caution:** Don't confuse activity with diversification. Having five different freelance jobs isn't diversification if they all depend on your time and health.

The streams also inform and strengthen each other. The expertise I develop ghostwriting gives me topics for books. The books establish credibility that attracts higher-paying ghostwriting clients. The editing work exposes me to different writing styles and industries that improve both my ghostwriting and my books.

This is different from having completely unrelated income streams that don't create any synergies. I've seen people try to combine dropshipping, cryptocurrency trading, and real estate investing because they heard diversification was important. But these activities require completely different skills and knowledge bases. You can't use success in one area to improve the others.

Good diversification means having streams that are different enough to provide stability but similar enough to create efficiencies and synergies.

The Ethics Test: Can You Sleep at Night?

One of the most important risk management tools is your own conscience. If an opportunity requires you to do things that make you uncomfortable, it's probably not sustainable long-term even if it's profitable short-term.

I learned this the hard way with affiliate marketing. I was making good money promoting other people's products, but I was constantly worried about whether the products I was promoting worked. I was getting paid to recommend things I'd never used to people I'd never met.

The pressure to promote higher-commission products was constant. The products that paid the most were usually the ones with the worst value propositions. Weight loss pills, get-rich-quick courses, investment schemes - stuff that preyed on people's desperation and insecurity.

I kept telling myself it wasn't my responsibility if people bought garbage based on my recommendations. I was just showing them what was available. They could make their own decisions. But I couldn't escape the feeling that I was taking advantage of people's trust for money.

The breaking point came when someone bought a $2,000 course based on my recommendation, realized it was worthless, and couldn't get a refund. I ended up refunding her money out of my own pocket because I couldn't live with knowing I'd helped someone get scammed.

> ★ **Pro Tip:** If you're constantly justifying your business practices to yourself, you're probably doing something you shouldn't be doing.

The ethics test is simple: Can you explain what you do to your family and friends without feeling embarrassed? Would you be comfortable if your business practices were featured in a newspaper article? Could you sleep well knowing that your success came at the expense of your customers?

This isn't about being perfect or never making mistakes. It's about choosing opportunities that align with your values and create genuine value for customers. It's about building something you can be proud of instead of something you have to hide.

Some people can compartmentalize their ethics and make money doing things they wouldn't recommend to friends. I'm not one of those people, and most people aren't either. The psychological cost of building a business that conflicts with your values is usually higher than the financial benefits.

There's also a practical element to ethics. Unethical businesses are unsustainable because they depend on finding new customers to replace the ones they've burned. Ethical businesses are sustainable because they create genuine value that leads to repeat customers and referrals.

Exit Strategies: When to Quit Something That's Not Working

Knowing when to quit is just as important as knowing when to scale. Most people are terrible at quitting because they get emotionally attached to ideas that aren't working and fall victim to the sunk cost fallacy.

The sunk cost fallacy is the tendency to continue investing in something because you've already invested in it, even when the evidence shows it's not working. You think, "I've already spent 100 hours on this, I can't quit now." But the 100 hours are gone regardless. The question is whether spending another 100 hours will be productive.

I spent six months trying to make money with online courses before admitting it wasn't working for me. I kept telling myself I just needed to improve my marketing, create better content, or find the right audience. The truth was that I didn't enjoy creating courses and wasn't good at marketing them. The time I was spending on courses would have been better spent on ghostwriting or book publishing.

> ■ **Danger Zone:** Don't let pride or sunk costs keep you trapped in opportunities that aren't working. Cutting losses is a skill, not a failure.

Here are the warning signs that it's time to quit an income stream:

Your hourly rate is consistently below minimum wage. If you're making less per hour than you could make at McDonald's, you're not building a business - you're volunteering for a company that doesn't value your time.

You dread working on it. If you avoid working on something because it's boring, stressful, or unpleasant, it's probably not sustainable long-term. Life is too short to spend your time on work you hate.

The market is moving against you. If competition is increasing, prices are dropping, and customer acquisition is getting harder despite your best efforts, the opportunity might be dying. Sometimes it's better to pivot to something new instead of fighting a losing battle.

You can't scale beyond your personal time investment. If the only way to make more money is to work more hours, you're still trading time for money, just without the employer. The goal is income that grows without requiring proportionally more of your hours.

The business model requires you to compromise your ethics. If success requires doing things that make you uncomfortable or that you wouldn't recommend to friends, find a different opportunity.

You're not learning or growing. If you've been doing something for months without getting better at it or learning new skills, it's probably not the right fit for your abilities or interests.

The key to successful quitting is setting criteria in advance. Before you start any new income stream, decide what success looks like and what failure looks like. How much time will you invest before expecting results? What metrics will you track? What would convince you that it's time to move on?

Having clear criteria makes the decision less emotional. Instead of "I think this might work if I just try harder," you can say "I committed to testing this for three months and tracking these metrics. The metrics show it's not working, so it's time to quit."

> **▲ Caution:** Don't quit too quickly, but don't persist too long either. Most income streams take 3-6 months to show real results, but if there's no progress after 6 months, it's probably time to try something else.

Quitting failed experiments frees up time and energy for opportunities that might work. The goal isn't to never fail - the goal is to fail fast and cheap when you're going to fail, and scale hard when you find something that works.

Remember: every successful entrepreneur has a graveyard of failed projects behind them. The difference between successful and unsuccessful entrepreneurs isn't that successful ones never fail. It's that they quit failing projects quickly and double down on successful projects aggressively.

Your willingness to walk away from opportunities that aren't working is what gives you the freedom to find opportunities that will work.

Scams Targeting Freelancers

Freelancing attracts predatory operators the same way any place with money and desperate people does. Not all of them are running outright fraud. The hard scams like the overpayment scheme and the content harvesting operation are covered earlier in this chapter. What follows are the extraction schemes that are technically legal but designed to take your money through manufactured urgency, inflated social proof, and exploitation of the sunk cost instinct. They are harder to spot than outright fraud because they offer real value, just not nearly as much as they charge for it.

The Webinar-to-Course Funnel

This one isn't a fraud in the legal sense. It's a marketing machine designed to extract money from people who are trying to learn how to make money. Understanding how it works makes it easy to use these events without getting used by them.

The structure is consistent. A free webinar (sometimes called a masterclass, workshop, or training) is promoted heavily through social media. The host is a successful entrepreneur, freelancer, or coach who has "cracked the code" on some income stream. The first 45 minutes is genuine content: real information, useful frameworks, specific examples. It's good enough that you trust the presenter and feel you're getting value. The last 15-20 minutes pivots to a pitch for a course, coaching program, or mastermind that costs anywhere from $297 to $10,000. The offer is available only at a special price for the next 24-48 hours. Urgency is manufactured. Testimonials appear. A payment plan is offered.

The economics of this model mean the free content has to be good enough to earn trust, but the real content, the specific implementation details, the proprietary systems, and the access to the presenter, is held back for the paid tier. This is not inherently dishonest. But it creates a predictable pattern: the free content tells you what, the paid program tells you how, and the how is often available elsewhere for less or for free if you're willing to look.

How to use webinars without overpaying for them. Attend for the free content and take notes. Write down the key concepts and look them up independently before buying anything. If the presenter is legitimate, their ideas will be findable in books, articles, or other sources. The 24-hour urgency is almost always fake. The same offer will be available next week, or a comparable one will exist from someone else. If you're genuinely considering a course or program, search for reviews from people who completed it, not testimonials the presenter selected.

> ★ **Pro Tip:** The legitimate use of a webinar is intelligence gathering. You find out whether this person actually knows what they're talking about, whether the framework resonates with your situation, and whether the paid program might be worth investigating further. The illegitimate use is letting the manufactured urgency and social proof of a live event override your normal judgment about a $2,000 purchase.

The Fake Testimonial Economy

Every course, coaching program, and platform in this space is covered in testimonials. Most of them are real. Some of them are not. Understanding the difference protects you from making expensive decisions based on manufactured social proof.

Red flags in testimonials: first name and last initial only with no verifiable profile. Video testimonials from people with no searchable online presence. Income claims with no context, no mention of time invested, starting point, expenses, or whether the result was repeated. Testimonials that all sound similar in structure and language, suggesting they were coached or templated. Screenshots of earnings that could be edited in seconds using browser developer tools.

The test for a testimonial is whether it is verifiable. A testimonial from someone with a real LinkedIn profile, a real business, and a specific result that matches what they actually do is meaningful. A testimonial from "Sarah M., stay-at-home mom, Florida" is not.

The Coaching Upsell Ladder

The coaching industry has developed a reliable extraction mechanism. It starts with a free lead magnet (a PDF, a video series, a quiz result) that gets you onto an email list. Then a low-ticket offer: a $47 course, a $97 workshop. If you buy, you're moved to a higher-ticket offer: a $997 program. If you buy that, you're invited to apply for a mastermind or coaching package at $5,000-$25,000. Each step builds commitment and sunk cost. The logic is: you've already invested this much, the next level is where the real results are.

This ladder works because each step feels justified by the previous one. You bought the $47 course and got some value, so the $997 program seems like a logical next step. But the returns per dollar diminish rapidly as you climb.

The $47 course often contains 80% of the actionable content. The $997 program adds community and live Q&A. The $10,000 mastermind adds access to the coach and peer networking, which has real value, but rarely $10,000 worth of value over what you already have.

Evaluate each level on its own merits, not as a continuation of previous purchases. The fact that you bought the entry-level product does not mean the next level will deliver proportional value. Ask specifically: what results have people at this tier achieved, how long did it take, and what did it cost them in total including time?

The Content Mill and Spec Work Trap

Some platforms and clients request "sample work" or "trial projects" as part of their vetting process. A legitimate trial engagement is paid, even if at a reduced rate. What some clients and platforms request is unpaid spec work: asking you to do real work under the pretense of evaluation, with no commitment to pay or hire you regardless of quality.

The tell is specificity. A legitimate skills test asks you to demonstrate a capability using a generic scenario. A spec work request asks you to produce something they could actually use: a custom logo for their real brand, a specific article for their actual publication, a real piece of code for their live product. If what they're asking you to create has value to them regardless of whether they hire you, it's spec work and it should be paid.

Content mills are a related trap. Platforms that pay per word or per article at rates below $0.05 per word are manufacturing content at scale using labor they've convinced themselves is voluntary. The economics don't work for the writer. A 1,000-word article at $0.03 per word pays $30. A competent writer who takes two hours to research and write it has earned $15 per hour before taxes. A writer who produces three such articles a day earns $90 a day. These platforms are not a path to freelance income. They are a mechanism for extracting writing labor at below-market rates by making writers feel they're building experience and clips.

Experience and clips have value. But a year spent writing for content mills produces neither the income nor the client relationships that advance a freelance career. If you need clips, write for publications that pay at least $0.25 per word, or create your own content and publish it yourself. The portfolio value of a well-placed article in a real publication outweighs fifty bylines on content farm websites.

The Quick Pattern Test

Most scams and predatory schemes share a small set of structural features. When you encounter any opportunity, run it through these quickly.

Does success require you to spend money before you can make money? Legitimate work does not charge you for the privilege of doing it. Starter kits, training fees, platform access fees, and certification requirements that funnel back to the person who recruited you are warning signs.

Is the income claim specific but unverifiable? Real results can be checked. If someone claims to make $15,000 a month from a strategy, you should be able to find independent verification, not just their own screenshots and their affiliates' testimonials. Vague claims ("some students make six figures") with no context about how many tried, how long it took, or what it cost are not evidence.

Does the urgency feel manufactured? Countdown timers, limited spots, one-time-only pricing: these are conversion tools, not genuine constraints. Real opportunities do not disappear if you take 48 hours to research them.

Does anything about the client or engagement not quite add up? Trust that instinct. Scammers rely on targets overriding their own discomfort because they want the opportunity to be real. If something feels off, look harder before you proceed.

■ **Danger Zone:** The most effective scams feel like opportunities that match exactly what you've been looking for. The emotional pull of finally finding the thing that will work is what makes people override their own skepticism. Slow down when an opportunity seems too well-timed, too easy, or too good. That feeling is the moment to verify more carefully, not less.

Part III: Implementation

Running It Like a Real Business

Most advice about freelancing is either overly optimistic ("make $10,000 your first month!") or unnecessarily pessimistic ("the gig economy is just exploitation!"). Both perspectives miss the reality that lies somewhere in between.

The truth is that building sustainable income streams through gig work is possible, but it takes longer than the optimists claim and offers more opportunity than the pessimists admit. Success requires honest assessment of time investment versus income potential, realistic expectations about growth timelines, and systems that prevent you from working yourself into the ground.

This chapter isn't about crushing dreams or lowering expectations. It's about building a foundation that can support long-term success instead of short-term hustle that leads to long-term burnout.

Most people fail not because they lack skills or opportunities, but because they approach it with unrealistic expectations and unsustainable practices. They optimize for quick wins instead of building systems. They chase every opportunity instead of focusing on what works. They ignore the business fundamentals that separate sustainable enterprises from temporary side hustles.

This framework helps you avoid those mistakes by forcing honest evaluation of opportunities, sustainable growth practices, and proper business foundations from day one.

Honest Time Investment vs. Income Potential Analysis

The biggest lie in the marketing around this is that you can make significant money with minimal time investment. "Work 10 hours a week and make $5,000 a month!" "Build passive income streams that require no maintenance!" "Replace your full-time salary working part-time hours!"

This is a mathematical impossibility for most people in most situations. If something sounds too good to be true in terms of time-to-income ratio, it probably is.

Real income potential analysis requires tracking actual time investment, not just the time you spend on billable work. Include time spent finding clients, marketing your services, handling administration, dealing with difficult customers, and managing your business finances.

When I started ghostwriting, I tracked every minute I spent on the business for the first six months. Writing time was only about 60% of my total time investment. The other 40% went to client acquisition, project management, invoicing, and business development. My effective hourly rate was much lower than my nominal rate once I included all these activities.

> ★ **Pro Tip:** Track your time for at least one month to understand where your hours go. Most people vastly underestimate the non-billable time required to run a service business.

Income from freelancing follows predictable patterns. The first few months are usually low-income, high-effort as you learn the business and build your client base.

Months 3-6 show gradual improvement as you get better at finding clients and delivering work efficiently. Months 6-12 are where you start seeing sustainable income if you've been building systems instead of just completing tasks.

People who quit in the first three months never see the income potential. People who work unsustainably in months 6-12 burn out just as things start working. The key is setting expectations that account for the learning curve and building practices that can be maintained long-term.

Income potential varies dramatically based on skills, market conditions, and execution quality. A ghostwriter can make anywhere from $10/hour to $200/hour depending on their expertise and client base. The same person can have drastically different results based on how they position themselves and which clients they pursue.

Don't base your income projections on best-case scenarios or success stories from people with different skills and circumstances. Base them on realistic assessments of your current capabilities and market conditions, with room for gradual improvement as you gain experience.

How to Evaluate if Something Is Worth Your Time

Every opportunity has an opportunity cost - the value of the best alternative you're giving up. Spending time on low-value work means not having time available for higher-value opportunities.

The evaluation framework starts with calculating your current effective hourly rate across all your income streams. Include all time invested in finding work, completing work, and managing your business. This gives you a baseline for comparing new opportunities.

If a new opportunity pays less than your current effective rate and doesn't offer clear paths to higher rates, it's probably not worth pursuing. If it pays more but requires skills you don't have, factor in the learning time required to become profitable.

> ■ **Danger Zone:** Don't chase opportunities just because they're available. Every hour spent on mediocre work is an hour not available for better opportunities.

Consider growth potential, not just immediate income. A low-paying opportunity that teaches valuable skills or connects you with high-value clients might be worth the short-term income sacrifice. A high-paying opportunity that's a dead end might not be worth the long-term cost.

I took on several low-paying ghostwriting projects early in my career because they were with executives in industries I wanted to understand better. The immediate pay was below my target rate, but the learning and networking opportunities led to much higher-paying work later.

Non-monetary factors matter too: schedule flexibility, skill development, portfolio building, relationship creation, and stress levels. A slightly lower-paying opportunity might be better if it offers more flexibility or less stress than higher-paying alternatives.

The evaluation should also consider fit with your existing business model. Opportunities that use your current skills and client relationships are usually better than opportunities that require starting from scratch in new areas.

> ▲ **Caution:** Be honest about what you enjoy and what you're good at. Money can't compensate for work that makes you miserable or plays to your weaknesses.

Building Sustainable Systems Without Burning Out

The hustle culture approach to this work is unsustainable. Working 80-hour weeks, sacrificing health and relationships for income, and constantly chasing the next opportunity leads to burnout that can take years to recover from.

Sustainable systems prioritize consistency over intensity. They're designed to work with your natural energy patterns and life constraints instead of demanding superhuman effort and sacrifice.

Start by identifying your productive hours and protecting them for high-value work. Don't schedule client calls during your best writing hours. Don't do administrative tasks when your brain is capable of creative work. Don't let urgent-but-unimportant tasks crowd out important-but-not-urgent activities.

Build buffer time into your schedules and deadlines. Projects always take longer than expected. Clients always have revision requests. Life always throws unexpected challenges at you. Systems that only work if everything goes perfectly will fail when reality intervenes.

I build 20% buffer time into all project estimates and deadlines. This allows me to handle revisions, deal with scope creep, and manage personal emergencies without missing commitments or working unsustainable hours.

Develop standard operating procedures for routine tasks. Email templates for common client communications. Checklists for project delivery.

Workflows for handling revisions and scope changes. Systems reduce decision fatigue and ensure consistent quality even when you're tired or distracted.

Set boundaries and communicate them clearly. Define your working hours and stick to them. Establish response time expectations for emails and messages. Create policies for handling rush requests and scope changes. Boundaries prevent client demands from consuming your entire life.

★ **Pro Tip:** Treat your systems like infrastructure investments. The time you spend building processes and templates pays dividends for years through increased efficiency and reduced stress.

The 80/20 Principle for Gig Economy Success

The Pareto Principle applies strongly to freelance work: roughly 80% of your results come from 20% of your efforts. The key is identifying which activities produce the highest returns and focusing your energy there.

For most service businesses, 80% of income comes from 20% of clients. The highest-paying, easiest-to-work-with clients who provide ongoing work and referrals. These clients should get priority attention and the majority of your relationship-building efforts.

I track client profitability not just by project fees, but by total relationship value including referrals and repeat work. My top 20% of clients generate about 75% of my income when you include the business they refer. These relationships get much more attention than one-off clients who pay similar project fees.

80% of your client acquisition probably comes from 20% of your marketing activities. Most marketing efforts generate little response, but a few channels or strategies produce consistent results. Double down on what works instead of constantly trying new approaches.

For me, LinkedIn networking and referrals from existing clients generate about 80% of new business. Content marketing, social media, and other strategies generate minimal results despite significant time investment. I've shifted my marketing focus accordingly.

80% of your problems probably come from 20% of your clients. The demanding, late-paying, scope-creeping clients who consume disproportionate time and energy. These relationships should be ended or restructured to prevent them from destroying your profitability and sanity.

> ▲ **Caution:** Don't confuse activity with results. Working harder on low-impact activities won't produce high-impact results.

The 80/20 principle also applies to skills development. A few core competencies probably drive most of your income potential. Focus skill development on areas that directly impact your earning ability rather than general professional development.

Ruthlessly eliminate or delegate activities that don't contribute to the vital 20%. Every hour spent on low-impact work is an hour not available for high-impact work. Efficiency in unimportant areas is still waste.

Practice Good Accounting and Follow the Law from Day One

Many freelancers and gig workers treat accounting and legal compliance as problems to solve later when they're making "real money." This approach creates expensive problems that are much harder to fix retroactively than to prevent from the beginning.

Good accounting starts with separating business and personal finances completely. Open a dedicated business checking account and use it exclusively for business income and expenses. This makes tax preparation much easier and provides clear documentation if you're ever audited.

Track every business expense, no matter how small. Office supplies, software subscriptions, equipment purchases, travel costs, client entertainment - all legitimate business expenses that reduce your taxable income. The few minutes spent recording expenses can save significant money at tax time.

I use simple accounting software (QuickBooks Simple Start) to track income and expenses automatically. Bank transactions are categorized as they occur, making tax preparation straightforward and ensuring I don't miss deductible expenses.

Save receipts for everything business-related. The IRS may want documentation for expenses, especially larger purchases or travel costs. Cloud storage makes receipt management easy - just photograph receipts with your phone and store them in organized folders.

Set aside money for taxes with every payment you receive. Freelancers and contractors don't have taxes withheld automatically, so you're responsible for saving money to pay quarterly estimated taxes and year-end tax obligations.

> ★ **Pro Tip:** Save 25-30% of every payment for taxes. Open a separate savings account for tax money and transfer the money immediately when you get paid.

Understand your state and local tax obligations. Some states have no income tax, others have high rates. Some cities have additional business taxes or licensing requirements. Research your specific obligations or consult with a local accountant.

Pay quarterly estimated taxes to avoid penalties. If you expect to owe more than $1,000 in taxes at year-end, you're required to make quarterly payments. Missing these payments results in penalties even if you pay the full amount by the tax deadline.

Avoid Debt if Possible - Bootstrap and Grow Organically

The temptation to use debt to grow your business faster is strong, especially when you see competitors with better equipment, larger teams, or more sophisticated marketing. But debt creates fixed monthly obligations that have to be paid regardless of your income fluctuations.

Income is inherently variable. You might make $5,000 one month and $1,000 the next month. Fixed debt payments don't adjust for income variability, creating cash flow problems during slow periods.

Bootstrap growth by reinvesting profits into business improvements rather than borrowing money to accelerate expansion. This takes longer but creates more sustainable growth that isn't dependent on external financing.

I've grown my business entirely through reinvested profits. When I needed a better computer, I saved money from client payments rather than financing the purchase. When I wanted to hire help, I waited until I had enough recurring income to cover the costs comfortably.

Organic growth forces you to prove business concepts before investing heavily in them. If you can't afford to test an idea with existing resources, it might not be a good idea. If you can prove an idea works with minimal investment, then scaling with profits makes sense.

> ■ **Danger Zone:** Business credit cards and equipment financing seem like "free money" but create fixed obligations that can kill your business during income downturns.

Debt can make sense for proven concepts with predictable returns. If you know that spending $1,000 on equipment will generate $2,000 in additional income over the next year, financing might be justified. But most business investments are less predictable than they appear.

The psychological burden of debt also affects decision-making. When you have monthly payments to make, you're more likely to take on bad clients or projects just to generate cash flow. This can damage your reputation and long-term income potential.

Cash flow management becomes much simpler without debt payments. Your monthly expenses are lower, so you can survive income fluctuations more easily. You have more flexibility to be selective about clients and projects.

Tax Implications and Business Structure Decisions

Most freelancers start as sole proprietors, which is the simplest business structure but not necessarily the best for tax purposes as income grows. Understanding your options helps you make informed decisions about when and how to change structures.

Sole proprietorship is the default structure for individual freelancers. All business income is reported on your personal tax return using Schedule C. You're responsible for both income taxes and self-employment taxes (Social Security and Medicare) on all profits.

Self-employment taxes are often the biggest surprise for new freelancers. The rate is 15.3% on top of regular income taxes, and it applies to all business profits. Employees split this cost with their employers, but freelancers pay the full amount.

Single-member LLCs provide liability protection without changing tax treatment. You're still taxed as a sole proprietor, but your personal assets have some protection from business liabilities. The cost and complexity are minimal in most states.

S-Corporation election can save self-employment taxes for profitable businesses. You pay yourself a reasonable salary (subject to employment taxes) and take additional profits as distributions (not subject to self-employment taxes). This only makes sense above certain income levels due to payroll processing costs.

> ▲ **Caution:** Don't change business structures just to save taxes. Structure changes have costs and complications that may outweigh tax savings for smaller businesses.

I started as a sole proprietor and switched to an LLC after my first year for liability protection. I'll consider S-Corp election if my income grows large enough to justify the additional complexity and costs.

Consult with a qualified accountant before making structure decisions. Tax laws are complex and change frequently. Generic advice may not apply to your specific situation, and mistakes can be expensive to correct.

Business structure affects more than just taxes. It impacts liability protection, business banking requirements, insurance needs, and legal compliance obligations. Consider all factors, not just immediate tax implications.

Record Keeping That Won't Bite You Later

Good record keeping protects you from IRS audits, client disputes, and business partnership problems. Poor record keeping creates expensive problems that could have been avoided with simple organizational systems.

Keep business records for at least seven years. The IRS generally has three years to audit returns, but the period extends to six years for substantial underreporting of income. Seven years provides a safe margin for most situations.

Document all client agreements in writing, even for small projects. Email confirmations of project scope, timelines, and payment terms prevent misunderstandings and provide evidence if disputes arise. Verbal agreements are hard to enforce and easy to misremember.

I send a brief email confirmation after every client conversation that outlines what we discussed and any decisions made. This creates a paper trail that prevents "I never agreed to that" situations later.

Track time spent on projects, even if you're not billing hourly. Time tracking helps you evaluate project profitability, estimate future projects accurately, and provide documentation if scope disputes arise.

Maintain organized files for each client and project. Include contracts, correspondence, invoices, payment records, and work products. Digital organization is fine, but make sure files are backed up and accessible if your computer fails.

Save all business communications for the duration of client relationships. Email threads, text messages, and project management system records provide context for decisions and protect you from disputes about what was agreed upon.

★ **Pro Tip:** Use descriptive file names and folder structures that make sense to someone else. If you're hit by a bus, your family or business partner should be able to find important documents.

Long-term Thinking: Reputation and Relationships Over Quick Wins

Freelancing rewards long-term thinking more than most people realize. While platforms and market conditions change rapidly, reputation and relationships provide stability that transcends any specific opportunity or trend.

Reputation takes time to build but pays dividends for years. Every satisfied client becomes a potential source of referrals. Every high-quality project becomes a portfolio piece that attracts better clients. Every professional relationship becomes a potential opportunity source.

I've gotten more work from referrals than from all marketing activities combined. Clients who hire me based on referrals are usually easier to work with, pay better rates, and provide clearer project requirements than clients acquired through other channels.

Reputation also provides protection against market changes. When platforms change algorithms or new competitors enter the market, established relationships and proven track records matter more than latest tactics or lowest prices.

Focus on delivering exceptional value rather than just meeting minimum requirements. Clients remember work that exceeds expectations and forget work that merely satisfies basic needs. The extra effort on each project compounds into reputation advantages that create pricing power.

Maintain relationships with past clients even after projects end. Send occasional updates about your business, share relevant industry information, and remember personal details they've shared. These relationships often lead to additional work or referrals years later.

▲ **Caution:** Don't sacrifice long-term reputation for short-term gains. One difficult client who damages your reputation can cost more than many good clients generate.

Managing Cash Flow While You're Building

The accounting section covers taxes and bookkeeping. This section covers something different: how to manage money practically when your income is irregular and still small. Most advice about freelance finances assumes you already have enough coming in. This is for the period before that.

The first thing to establish is your actual monthly floor, the minimum you need to cover rent, food, utilities, insurance, and debt payments. Not your comfortable number. The number below which things start breaking. Know this exactly. It is the number that determines whether a given month is survivable, and it is the benchmark against which you measure whether your building work is generating enough to rely on.

Until your building-work income has cleared your monthly floor for three consecutive months, don't treat it as income you can count on. Three months of consistent revenue at or above your floor is the minimum before you can make any significant financial decision based on that stream: reducing bridge work, increasing spending, or telling yourself the model is working. One good month is data. Three consecutive months is a pattern.

During the building phase, hold two separate buffers. The first is your operating buffer: one to two months of floor expenses in a checking account you don't touch except for bills. This is what prevents a slow month from becoming a crisis that forces you to take bad clients or make panicked decisions. The second is your tax buffer: 25-30% of every payment set aside immediately in a separate savings account. Self-employment tax is the most common financial shock for new freelancers. It is also completely predictable. Set the money aside before you see it as available.

Pay yourself a fixed amount each month rather than spending whatever came in. When income is irregular, spending tends to track the high months and the low months create shortfalls. A fixed monthly draw, set at roughly 60-70% of your average monthly revenue once you have three months of data, creates predictability even when income isn't. What you don't draw stays in the business account and builds toward the operating buffer.

★ **Pro Tip:** The moment your building-work income reliably clears your monthly floor, you have optionality. You can reduce bridge work, be more selective about clients, or experiment with raising rates. Before that moment, optionality is a goal, not a reality. Know which side of that line you're on.

The question of when to call the income stream "working" matters because people often call it too early. They have one strong month, reduce their bridge work, and then face a lean month without the buffer they needed. The three-month rule is conservative by design. Better to maintain bridge income one month longer than necessary than to pull it too soon and spend the next month in recovery.

Invest in skill development that increases your long-term value rather than just solving immediate problems. Learning skills that will be valuable for years beats learning tactics that might become obsolete quickly.

Think about where you want your business to be in 5-10 years and make decisions that move you toward that vision. Short-term optimization often conflicts with long-term strategy. Choose long-term whenever possible.

This isn't about being conservative or risk-averse. It's about being realistic about what works, honest about what doesn't, and strategic about building something sustainable.

Most failures come from unrealistic expectations, unsustainable practices, or poor business fundamentals. The framework helps you avoid these problems by forcing honest evaluation and systematic thinking about business building.

Success is possible, but it requires treating this like a real business with real systems, real accounting, and real long-term planning. The framework provides the structure to build something that lasts.

The experimentation method tells you what to test. This chapter tells you how to run the test, specifically what to do the week you decide to start. How to approach someone without it feeling like a pitch. How to set a price when you have no reference point. How to scope the first engagement small enough that someone says yes. And what to do when they do.

Most people skip this part. They understand the methodology, they have a candidate skill, they know they should test it, and then they stall. The stall usually comes down to three things: they don't know what to say, they don't know what to charge, and they don't know how to ask for the sale without feeling like they're begging. Those are solvable problems.

How to Make the First Approach

The first approach is not a pitch. If you frame it as a pitch, it feels like a pitch to you and to them, and pitches invite rejection. Frame it as a conversation about a problem you suspect they have.

The formula is simple: "I've been doing X for Y years and I'm starting to work with people outside my current role. I know [specific type of person] often struggles with [specific problem]. Is that something you deal with?" That's it. You're not offering anything yet. You're confirming that the problem exists for this specific person before you propose a solution.

When they say yes (and if you've picked the right person, they usually do), follow up with one question: "What does that cost you?" Cost in time, money, stress, whatever. You're not being nosy. You're finding out whether this problem is worth solving. If they can't answer that question, the problem isn't painful enough to pay someone to fix. If they answer it immediately and specifically, you have a customer.

The people to approach first are people who already know you. Former colleagues, neighbors, people in professional groups you belong to, people you've helped informally. You don't need to cold approach strangers for your first test. Your existing network almost certainly contains people with the problem you solve. The warm approach converts at a much higher rate and gives you cleaner signal about whether the problem is real.

> ★ **Pro Tip:** You're not asking anyone to do you a favor. You're asking if they have a problem you might be able to solve. Those are completely different conversations.

If you don't have a professional network yet (you're early in your career, you've worked service jobs, you changed fields), the warm-contact strategy has less to work with, and that's worth naming directly. In that case, the path to a first client runs through visibility rather than relationships. But visibility is not free work, and this distinction matters.

Never give your services away for free. It is almost impossible to convert someone who is accustomed to getting your work for nothing into a paying client, and they won't refer you to paying clients either, because in their mind you're the person who works for free. The only exception is a formal internship tied to academic credit, where the arrangement is defined and temporary. A free discovery call is also appropriate: a 30-minute conversation over Zoom to understand their problem and find out whether you can help. That's not giving your service away. You're not producing anything they keep. It's how you qualify the engagement before you price it, and it's how professionals in any field open a relationship. Outside of those two situations, free service is not generosity: it's a pricing decision that follows you.

What you give freely is your knowledge, not your deliverables. Pick one online community where the people you want to serve are already talking: a subreddit, a Facebook group for small business owners, a Discord for your target industry. Join committees or working groups. Answer questions in your area. Start posts with what you know or questions that open real discussions. Comment on other people's posts thoughtfully. Lead something when the opportunity comes up. Do all of this without asking for anything and without attaching a pitch. If you do graphic design, spend two weeks in an indie game dev community talking about art direction and file formats before you mention you take commissions. When you do eventually describe what you're offering, you're not a stranger; you're the person who contributed something useful last week. The first client comes from that, not from a cold pitch. It takes longer than calling a former colleague, but it builds from zero.

> **★ Pro Tip:** Contribute without attaching a pitch. Most people join a community and immediately start angling. The ones who get clients are the ones who showed up and added something first. When you've been useful for two weeks, describing what you offer isn't a pitch; it's a natural next step.

How to Set a Price With No Reference Point

Pricing your first engagement is the thing that stops most people. They don't know what to charge, so they either undercharge dramatically or they stall trying to figure out the right number.

Here is how to find a starting number when you have no reference point. Estimate how long the engagement will take in hours. Multiply by the lowest rate you'd accept per hour for professional work, not minimum wage, but not your dream rate either. The number you get is your floor. Then find two or three people or companies who offer something similar and see what they charge. You don't have to match them, but you need to know where the market is. If your floor is significantly below market, raise it. If it's above market, either you've scoped too large or your rate expectation is off.

For most skill-based services, the first engagement should be priced to get a yes, not to maximize revenue. That doesn't mean working for free. Free work validates nothing, as the methodology chapter explains. It means pricing at a level where the client feels the risk is low and you get clean data about whether people will pay at all. You'll raise rates after you have two or three paying clients and a clearer sense of what the work requires.

When someone pushes back on your price, ask before you discount: "What were you expecting to pay?" This tells you a lot. If they expected significantly less, you may be in the wrong market or the wrong tier of client. If they expected about the same but were trying their luck, you know your price is right and you can hold it. Discounting before you know why they're pushing back is almost always a mistake.

■ **Danger Zone:** Underpricing to get your first client attracts clients who bought on price. Those clients are the hardest to work with and the least likely to refer you to anyone useful.

There is a specific pricing problem that affects technical freelancers: engineers, analysts, IT specialists, financial consultants, anyone whose work involves expertise the client doesn't fully understand. The floor-rate-times-hours method gets you started, but it doesn't solve the harder question: how do you hold a rate when the client doesn't know enough to evaluate whether you're worth it?

The answer is to price the problem, not the service. A client who doesn't understand what you do will always compare your rate to the cheapest alternative they can find, because price is the only variable they know how to evaluate. A client who understands what the problem costs them will compare your rate to that number, and your rate will almost always look reasonable by comparison.

In practice this means the pricing conversation comes after the problem conversation, not before it. Before you quote anything, get specific about what the unresolved problem is costing the client: in time, in money, in risk, in rework, in whatever the relevant currency is for their situation. Ask directly. "What does it cost you when this goes wrong?" or "How long does your team spend dealing with this every month?" You're not being nosy. You're finding the number your quote needs to be smaller than.

Once you have that number, your quote is a fraction of it. A client who loses $15,000 a quarter to a problem you can fix will rarely resist a $4,000 engagement fee. A client who can't name what the problem costs them, who says "it's just annoying" or "it takes a while," either doesn't have a painful enough problem to pay to solve, or doesn't trust you enough yet to tell you. Either way, you don't have a client. More conversation first.

The second piece is scope clarity. Technical clients often resist rates not because they think you're overcharging but because they can't see what they're buying. A vague engagement ("I'll help you improve your data pipeline") sounds expensive because it's unbounded. A specific engagement ("I'll audit your current pipeline, identify the three highest-risk failure points, and deliver a written remediation plan with implementation timeline") sounds like a product with a price tag. Same work, completely different conversation. Specificity makes the value visible to someone who can't evaluate the expertise behind it.

> ★ **Pro Tip:** When a technical client pushes back on your rate, the first question is usually the wrong one. Don't immediately ask what they expected to pay. Ask first: "Can you help me understand what you're comparing this to?" The answer tells you whether they've found a cheaper alternative (positioning problem), don't understand the scope (clarity problem), or just haven't connected the fee to the cost of the problem (framing problem). Each one has a different response.

Scoping the First Engagement

The first engagement should be small enough that a stranger will say yes to it. Not your full service. Not an ongoing retainer. One concrete thing with a clear deliverable, a defined scope, and a specific price.

The bookkeeping example in the methodology chapter gets this right: not "I'll manage your books," but "I'll reconcile one month of transactions for $75." One thing. Specific price. Clear output. A stranger can say yes to that because the risk is contained. If the work is good, you discuss what comes next. If it isn't, they lost $75 and you learned something.

Apply this to whatever you're testing. If you're testing HR consulting, don't offer a "consulting relationship." Offer to review one job description and rewrite it. If you're testing technical writing, offer one FAQ document or one process guide. If you're testing coaching, offer one 90-minute session to work through one specific decision they're stuck on. The small scope reduces the friction to getting started and forces you to define what you actually deliver before you have to deliver it.

Avoid retainers and ongoing arrangements for the first engagement. Those require trust that doesn't exist yet. Earn the trust with a small, well-scoped piece of work first. The client will raise the ongoing conversation themselves if the work is good.

The First Conversation

If the approach conversation goes well, you'll get to a point where the client is interested but nothing is agreed. Here is what that conversation needs to accomplish: confirm the problem, confirm they want help, agree on a specific deliverable, agree on a price, agree on a timeline. That's the whole list.

Don't leave the conversation without those five things settled. Not because you're being pushy, but because "let's stay in touch" is not a client. An interested person who hasn't agreed to anything specific will be an interested person indefinitely. Getting to a specific agreement is how you find out whether the interest is real.

The close doesn't have to be a hard sell. It can be as simple as: "If you want to move forward, I can have [specific deliverable] to you by [specific date] for [price]. Want me to send you a quick confirmation email so we're on the same page?" An email confirmation is not a contract (though a contract is better if the engagement is large). It's a record that something was agreed, which protects both parties from misremembering.

> ★ **Pro Tip:** The person who sends the summary email after a conversation controls the record of what was agreed. Always be that person.

After the First Yes

When someone says yes, two things happen simultaneously. You have to deliver the work. And you have to keep your pipeline moving.

Most people getting their first client stop all outreach because they're busy with the work. This is how the feast-or-famine cycle starts. The project ends, there is nothing in the pipeline, and you start from zero. Even when you're busy with your first engagement, keep approaching two or three people per week. It doesn't have to be formal. It can be a message to a former colleague, a comment on someone's LinkedIn post about a problem you solve, a question in a community you belong to. The work is to keep the signal going while you deliver.

Deliver the first engagement as well as you can, but don't over-deliver to the point where you've underpriced yourself for the actual work required. If the engagement took twice as long as you estimated, that's pricing data for the next one. If it took half as long, you either scoped incorrectly or you're faster than you thought. Either way, you now have real information that you didn't have before.

At the end of the engagement, ask two questions. First: "Is there anything you wished this included that it didn't?" This tells you whether the scope was right. Second: "Do you know anyone else who deals with this kind of problem?" Not "can you refer me," since that puts them in an awkward position. Asking whether they know anyone else is a low-pressure way to open the referral conversation. If they do, they'll usually say so.

One paying customer who is satisfied is worth more than ten people who are "interested." That first client is proof that the model works at small scale. It's validation that someone will pay you, that the deliverable is real, and that you can do the work. Everything after that is refinement.

▲ **Caution:** Treat every first engagement as a learning engagement, not a showcase engagement. You're finding out what this work actually requires, not proving you've already figured it out.

If Your Timeline Is Short

Everything in this chapter assumes you have time to run a test, learn from it, and iterate. If you just lost your job and rent is due in six weeks, that assumption is wrong. The execution sequence is the same, but the priorities are different.

Start with the smallest possible version of a skill you already have and the warmest contacts you already know.

Not the most exciting candidate on your inventory list, but the one that can generate money fastest. That usually means a skill directly connected to work you've already been paid for, offered to someone who already knows your work. A former employer who needs contract help in exactly the area you just left. A colleague who has seen you solve the problem you're offering to solve. You are not starting from zero with these people. The trust already exists. The conversation is shorter, the close is faster, and the timeline from first approach to first payment is days rather than weeks.

When your runway is short, skip the most ambitious scope and go straight to the smallest deliverable someone will pay for. Not because you can't do more, but because smaller scope means faster yes, faster start, and faster payment. A two-hour consulting call someone will book this week beats a three-month project that takes two weeks to negotiate and another month to invoice.

Parallel-track the survival and bridge work from the If You Just Lost Your Job chapter with the execution steps here. Survival work keeps the electricity on while you run your first real test. Bridge work gives you a floor while you build. The execution steps in this chapter are not a substitute for that sequence. They run alongside it. The goal is to get your first building-work customer while the bridge income is covering your basics, so you're not making the first approach from a position of desperation. Desperation shows in negotiations, affects pricing decisions, and pushes you toward accepting clients and terms you shouldn't accept.

Two things to skip entirely when time is short. First, skip the inventory exercise and go straight to your most obvious, most proven skill, the one you've been paid for before. The inventory is valuable when you have time to think. When you don't, you already know what you're testing. Second, skip the market research phase and price based on your floor rate. You can refine pricing after you have your first client. Right now you need the client.

★ **Pro Tip:** The difference between someone who builds something real in a crisis and someone who doesn't is usually one conversation. The person who sends three messages to warm contacts on the first day has a completely different outcome than the person who spends that day researching their options. Research is procrastination when your timeline is six weeks.

If your timeline is longer (you have a job, you have savings, you have runway), the rest of this chapter applies as written. Run the inventory, research the market, scope carefully, iterate. You have the luxury of finding the best opportunity rather than the fastest one. Use it. The people who build the most durable income streams are almost always the ones who started before they had to.

When a Test Doesn't Work: Diagnosing Before Moving On

The methodology says kill what doesn't work and move on. That's right, but moving on without understanding why it didn't work means the next test is a guess. Before you abandon a candidate, run through four questions. The answer usually tells you whether the problem is the idea itself or one fixable variable.

First: did anyone confirm the problem exists? If you approached three people and none of them recognized the problem you were solving, the problem may not be real for this population, or you may be describing it in terms they don't recognize. Try describing the same problem differently to two or three more people before you kill the idea. If they still don't recognize it, the problem isn't there.

Second: did anyone confirm the problem exists but decline to pay? This is different from the first case and more informative. It means the problem is real but either the price is wrong, the deliverable isn't compelling, or they're solving it another way already. Ask directly: "What would it take for this to be worth paying for?" or "How are you handling it now?" The answer tells you whether to reprice, rescope, or move on.

Third: did someone say yes but not follow through? A verbal yes that doesn't convert to payment or a signed-off email is not a yes. It's a polite no. This usually means the problem isn't painful enough to prioritize, the scope felt too large, or you didn't get to a specific agreement in the conversation. Go back and try a smaller, more concrete offering with the next person.

Fourth: did you get one paying customer but couldn't get a second? This is the best kind of failure. It means the model works but something about your approach, your market, or your positioning isn't scaling. Ask the person who paid you who else they know with the same problem. Ask them what made them say yes. That conversation is worth more than another round of cold approaches.

■ **Danger Zone:** "It didn't work" is not a diagnosis. Before you move to the next candidate, know specifically which of the four cases above applies. That knowledge is what makes the next test faster.

If you've run through all four questions and the answer is genuinely that the problem doesn't exist, the market is too thin, or you don't have the right skill for the right buyer, then move on. That's not failure. That's the methodology working exactly as designed. You spent a week finding out something that would have taken six months to discover any other way.

Writing a Statement of Work

A confirmation email says something was agreed. A Statement of Work (SOW) says what was agreed, with enough specificity that neither party can reasonably claim they understood something different. For a small, one-time engagement with a warm contact, a confirmation email is usually enough. For anything ongoing, anything with multiple deliverables, anything involving a client you don't know, or anything over a few hundred dollars, you need an SOW. The cost of writing one is an hour. The cost of not having one, when a dispute arises, is considerably higher.

An SOW doesn't have to be a legal document. It doesn't need to be formatted like a contract or written in lawyer language. It needs to answer seven questions clearly enough that if you and the client read it six months from now, you'd both understand exactly what was agreed.

What Goes in a Basic SOW

The first question is what you're delivering. Not a general description, but the specific output. For a ghostwriter, this means word count, format, number of drafts, and what costs extra. For a bookkeeper, it means which accounts, which period, what format the deliverable takes, and whether tax preparation is included or separate. For an AI consultant helping a small business implement tools, it means which tools, what configuration work is included, whether training the client's team is in scope, and what ongoing support if any is covered. Every item that's explicitly excluded saves a future argument. The things clients assume are included are almost always the things you assumed were excluded.

The second question is what the client is responsible for. Most project delays and disputes trace back to client-side failures: late feedback, missed meetings, slow approvals, incomplete information. Your SOW should state what you need from the client and what happens when you don't get it. For a bookkeeper: "Client will provide bank statements and receipts within five business days of each month's close. Delays in providing source documents will delay deliverables accordingly." For an AI implementation project: "Client will provide access to required systems within three business days of signing. Consultant is not responsible for delays caused by access restrictions." For a writing project: "If no written feedback is received within seven days of draft delivery, that draft will be considered accepted." That last clause prevents a client from sitting on a deliverable for months and then saying it doesn't meet the brief.

The third question is payment. State the total, state when it's due, state what happens if it's late. For larger projects, milestone-based payment is better than a single payment at completion, since it protects you from finishing the work and not getting paid, and it protects the client from paying everything upfront. Milestone payments tie each invoice to a specific deliverable: the outline, the first draft, the revision. Work on the next milestone begins when the previous invoice is paid. This is standard professional practice, not a sign of distrust. A deposit before work begins (25% is typical) signals that the client is serious and covers your time if they disappear after the first meeting.

The fourth question is what happens with revisions and changes. Define what one revision includes. State that major changes outside the original plan require a scope discussion before you proceed. Without this language, a client can request indefinite changes and you have no basis for declining or billing for the extra work. For an AI project, this might mean: "Up to two rounds of configuration adjustments based on testing feedback are included. Changes to the underlying tools, platforms, or business requirements after implementation begins constitute a scope change." For a writing engagement: "One full revision based on client feedback is included. Requests involving major structural changes after outline approval will be treated as new scope."

The fifth question is who owns the work. For most service engagements, ownership transfers to the client upon final payment. State this explicitly. If you retain any rights, such as to use the work as a portfolio sample, a case study, or an anonymized example, specify that and get the client's agreement in writing. For AI and software work, ownership of custom code, models, or configurations should be addressed clearly. Work built on third-party tools may have licensing constraints that limit what the client can do with it. Note those limitations in the SOW so there are no surprises later.

The sixth question is what happens if the project stops. Either party should be able to exit with reasonable written notice, 30 days is standard. State that completed, paid-for work transfers to the client regardless of how the engagement ends. State what happens to unpaid invoices. If the client goes silent for an extended period, state how long before the project is considered abandoned and what you're entitled to retain. A clean termination clause prevents an unfinished project from becoming a legal dispute.

Indemnification Is Not Optional

The seventh question is liability, and this one is not negotiable, regardless of what type of work you do.

An indemnification clause states that if your work causes harm to a third party, the client, not you, bears the legal and financial responsibility for content, claims, or outcomes that originate from information the client provided. This matters in every field, and the stakes vary by discipline.

For a writer or ghostwriter: if a client asks you to include claims that turn out to be false, defamatory, or infringing on someone else's copyright, and a lawsuit results, you need the client to indemnify you. You wrote what they asked you to write based on what they told you was accurate. That is their liability, not yours.

For a bookkeeper or accountant: if a client provides you with incomplete, inaccurate, or falsified records, and a tax authority later determines there are errors or fraud, you need the client to indemnify you. You worked with the information you were given. The client is responsible for the accuracy of their own records.

For an AI consultant or implementer: if you build a system based on client requirements and that system produces outputs the client uses in ways that harm their customers or violate regulations, you need the client to indemnify you. You built what was specified. The client decided how to use it and is responsible for ensuring their use complies with applicable law.

The common thread across all three cases: you are a service provider executing work based on client instructions and client-provided information. You are not the decision-maker, the end-user, or the person accountable for how the output is applied. The indemnification clause formalizes that distinction. Without it, a client can point to you when something goes wrong, even when the failure originated entirely on their side.

A matching clause that belongs alongside indemnification: cap your liability at the total fees paid under the agreement. You cannot make warranties about commercial outcomes, legal compliance in the client's jurisdiction, or third-party behavior that you don't control. State that explicitly. A ghostwriter cannot guarantee a book will sell. A bookkeeper cannot guarantee a client will avoid an audit. An AI implementer cannot guarantee a tool will perform identically across all future use cases. What you can guarantee is that you'll do the work professionally and to the specification agreed. Your liability is limited to that.

■ **Danger Zone:** Clients sometimes push back on indemnification language, particularly smaller clients who are signing their first professional services agreement. Don't remove it. Explain it plainly: this clause says that if you give me wrong information and something goes wrong because of it, that's your problem to solve, not mine. Any reasonable client accepts that. A client who won't accept it is signaling something worth paying attention to.

When You Need More Than a Basic SOW

For small engagements, a few hours, a single deliverable, a client you know well, a one-page document covering the seven questions is sufficient. As engagements get larger, longer, or more complex, the SOW should get more specific.

For ongoing retainer relationships, add a clause about what happens if either party wants to change the scope month to month. For work involving sensitive client information, financial records, proprietary business data, personal information about the client's customers, add a confidentiality clause and state how long you'll retain their data and how you'll dispose of it. For AI work touching regulated industries like healthcare, finance, or legal services, consider whether you need to consult an attorney before signing, because compliance obligations in those fields can create liability you don't want to assume unknowingly.

You don't need a lawyer to write a basic SOW. You need to write clearly and cover the seven questions. Templates are available online for most common service types. After a few engagements, you'll develop your own standard language that you refine over time. The first SOW you write will be imperfect. Write it anyway. The discipline of putting the agreement in writing, before work starts, every time, is the practice. The language improves with experience.

> ★ **Pro Tip:** Send the SOW before you start, not after. An SOW sent after work begins is a document the client is less motivated to read carefully, because they're already getting what they want. The SOW signing is also the moment the engagement officially starts. Make it a clean sequence: SOW signed, deposit received if applicable, work begins.

The confirmation email and the SOW serve different purposes. The confirmation email is fast, informal, and right for small tests and first engagements with known contacts. The SOW is formal, specific, and right for anything you'd be seriously upset about losing. As your engagements get larger and your clients become less familiar, the balance shifts toward the SOW almost every time.

When Things Go Wrong

Almost every freelancer in their first year encounters at least one of three situations: a client who doesn't pay, a client who expands the scope without agreeing to pay more, and a client who disputes the work after delivery. None of these have to be catastrophic if you know what to do before they happen.

The Non-Paying Client

Prevention is better than collection. Before starting any paid engagement, send a written confirmation (email is sufficient) that states what you're delivering, the price, and the payment timeline. For new clients you don't know, ask for 50% upfront. Not because you don't trust them, but because it establishes immediately that you operate like a business, and it filters out clients who were never serious about paying.

When a payment is late, contact the client the day after it was due. Not a week later. A short, neutral message: "Just following up, the invoice for [project] was due yesterday. Let me know if there's anything you need from me to process it." Most late payments are administrative, not malicious. This message usually resolves it within 24 hours.

If a second follow-up at one week produces nothing, escalate the language slightly: "The invoice for [project] is now [X] days overdue. Please let me know by [specific date] when I can expect payment, or whether there's a problem I can help resolve." Setting a specific date creates a deadline without being aggressive.

For amounts under your state's small claims limit (typically $5,000-$10,000), small claims court is a realistic option and doesn't require a lawyer. The filing process is straightforward, and the existence of your written confirmation email is usually sufficient evidence. Many non-paying clients pay immediately when they receive a small claims notice, before the case is ever heard. Your written confirmation email is your evidence. This is why you always send it.

■ **Danger Zone:** Don't threaten legal action and then not follow through. Empty threats train clients to ignore you. If you say you're filing in small claims, file.

Scope Creep

Scope creep is when a client asks for more than what was agreed without acknowledging that more work requires more money. It is the most common reason early freelancers undercharge and overdeliver. It happens gradually, one small addition at a time, and by the time the project ends, you've done 40% more work than you were paid for.

The fix is a boundary you set at the beginning, not the end. When a client asks for something outside the original scope, respond before doing it: "Happy to include that. That's outside what we originally agreed, so I'll send you a quick addendum for [price] and we can get started once that's confirmed." This does three things. It makes the boundary visible. It gives the client the choice to approve or decline. And it establishes that your time has a price, which clients who are worth keeping will respect.

For small additions, things that will take you 15 minutes, use your judgment. Building some goodwill with a good client is worth more than billing every five-minute request. The goal is to be reasonable without being exploitable. The pattern to watch for is accumulation: if a client's small requests happen every week, they're not small anymore.

★ **Pro Tip:** Your written confirmation email is your scope document. When a client says "I thought this included X," you have a record of exactly what was agreed. Refer to it calmly and without accusation. Most scope disputes are genuine misunderstandings, not bad faith.

Work That Gets Disputed

A client who says the work doesn't meet the brief has either a legitimate complaint or a buyer's remorse problem. The distinction matters because the response is different.

A legitimate complaint means the work genuinely doesn't match what was agreed. This is on you to fix, even if it takes more time than expected. The fastest way through it is to ask the client to be specific: "Can you tell me exactly what's missing or what needs to change?" A client with a real complaint will have specific answers. Fix what they identify, confirm the fix meets the brief, and move on. Don't argue about whether the original work was good. That conversation has no good outcome.

Buyer's remorse looks different. The client can't articulate what's wrong. Or what's wrong keeps shifting as you address each concern. Or the complaints start after you ask for payment. In this case, refer to the written confirmation and the specific deliverable you agreed to. "Based on what we agreed in [email], the deliverable was [X]. I believe what I've delivered matches that. I'm happy to make the specific changes you described. Can you send those in writing so I make sure I address everything?" Putting the changes in writing slows down moving-target complaints and creates a record of what was finally agreed.

For your first few clients, err toward generosity. Your reputation is worth more than the extra hour it takes to revise something. But track what happened. A pattern of disputes with one client is information about whether to work with them again. A pattern across multiple clients might mean your scoping conversations need to be more specific.

How to Raise Your Rates

The book has said more than once that you'll raise rates after you have a few clients. Here is how to actually do it.

Raising Rates With New Clients

The simplest way to raise rates with new clients is to charge more. Quote the new rate when you price the engagement. You don't need to explain or justify it. Most clients have no idea what you charged your previous clients. They only know what you quote them now.

The signal that tells you a rate increase is warranted: you're getting yeses too easily. If every prospect agrees to your rate without hesitation or negotiation, your rate is probably below market. A small amount of pushback (not rejection, just pushback) means your pricing is in the right range. If you lose an occasional prospect on price, that's normal and fine. You can't know where the ceiling is until you've hit it.

Raise rates in steps, not jumps. Going from $50/hour to $150/hour in one move creates sticker shock and makes it hard to distinguish a pricing problem from a positioning problem. Going from $50 to $70, testing that for a few engagements, then moving to $90 gives you data at each step about what the market will bear.

Raising Rates With Existing Clients

This is the conversation most freelancers avoid, which means most freelancers get stuck at their original rate indefinitely while their costs go up and their skills improve. The conversation is not as difficult as it feels.

Give existing clients advance notice, 30 to 60 days is standard. Frame it matter-of-factly, not apologetically: "I wanted to let you know that starting [date], my rate for [type of work] will be [new rate]. I've appreciated working with you and wanted to give you plenty of notice to adjust if needed." That's the whole message. You don't need to explain the increase or justify it. Rates go up. Everyone understands this.

Most clients who value your work will accept the increase. Some will push back. If a client pushes back and you want to keep them, you can offer to hold the current rate for a fixed period ("I can hold your current rate through [date] if that helps with planning"), but don't abandon the increase entirely. Agreeing to never raise rates with a client means you've effectively taken a pay cut every year as your costs increase.

Some clients will leave when you raise rates. This is usually fine and sometimes good. Clients who were only with you because of price are not your best clients. The clients worth keeping are the ones who value your work enough to pay a fair rate for it. A rate increase is a natural filter that tends to leave you with better clients.

> ★ **Pro Tip:** The best time to raise rates is when you have more work than you can comfortably handle. Full capacity is the clearest signal that demand exceeds supply at your current price. That's the definition of when to raise prices.

A practical benchmark: if you haven't raised rates in 12 months and your work has improved, your rate has effectively decreased relative to your value. Build rate reviews into your calendar the same way you build tax payments in. Once a year, evaluate whether your current rate reflects what you now know and what the market will bear. Then adjust.

Getting Paid: Payment Platforms and How to Protect Yourself

How you collect money matters more than most freelancers think about until they get burned. The platform you use determines who can pay you, what it costs, how fast you get the money, and critically, what happens when a client disputes a payment. This chapter covers the two platforms most commonly used by US-based freelancers, what each one is good for, and the protection and risk picture on each.

First, the rule that applies regardless of platform: payment funds should go into a dedicated account that is not your primary checking or savings account. Not because clients are dishonest, but because chargebacks and refunds are processed directly from whatever account your payment platform is linked to. If that account is your savings, a disputed payment can pull from your savings. A dedicated payment account, a separate checking account used only for business income, puts a firewall between your payment activity and your personal finances. It also makes bookkeeping cleaner and tax preparation simpler. Set this up before you accept your first payment.

Zelle

Zelle is a bank-to-bank transfer network built into most US banking apps. It is free for both sender and receiver, transfers are typically instant or within minutes, and there are no transaction fees. For US-based clients who bank with major institutions, it is the cleanest and fastest option available. The money arrives directly in your account with no intermediary holding it.

The limitation is geography: Zelle is US only. If a client is outside the United States, Zelle is not an option.

The more important thing to understand about Zelle is how it handles disputes, or more precisely, how it doesn't. Zelle does not have a chargeback process. Transactions are treated like cash: once the money is sent to an enrolled recipient, it is final and cannot be reversed by Zelle. This is actually good news for you as a service provider. A client cannot file a chargeback with Zelle the way they can with a credit card payment.

The protection that does exist on Zelle is narrow and only covers genuine fraud, meaning unauthorized transactions where someone else accessed the client's account without their knowledge. Under Regulation E of the Electronic Fund Transfer Act, clients have up to 60 days from their bank statement date to report an unauthorized transaction, and their bank is required to investigate. If the bank determines the transaction was genuinely unauthorized, they may reverse it. But if a client authorized the payment and later decides they want the money back, even if they claim they were scammed, Zelle offers no recourse. That is the client's problem, not yours.

Some banks allow customers to file a dispute on Zelle transactions up to 120 days after the transaction, but the standard available to most users is the 60-day Regulation E window, and recovery on these disputes is not guaranteed. The practical implication: Zelle payments to enrolled recipients are about as final as payments get in the digital world. This is a feature, not a bug, for freelancers.

One practical limitation: Zelle transfer limits are set by individual banks, not by Zelle itself, and vary widely. Limits vary by bank and are set on daily and monthly cycles, not weekly. Most major banks allow personal account holders to send $3,000 to $3,500 per day, with business accounts reaching $15,000 per day or more. New accounts are often capped lower for the first 60 days. For a $5,000 invoice from a client at a major bank, they may need to send $3,500 on day one and the balance the following day once their limit resets. This is common and clients understand it once you explain it. State it in your SOW for larger engagements: "For invoices that exceed your client's daily Zelle limit, payment may require multiple transfers across consecutive days. Payment is considered received when all transfers are complete." No processing fee on a split Zelle payment versus a card fee on the full amount is still a clear win for both parties.

Stripe

Stripe accepts credit and debit cards from clients anywhere in the world. It is the right choice for international clients, clients who prefer to pay by card, or any situation where Zelle isn't an option. The tradeoff is cost and chargeback exposure.

Stripe charges approximately 2.9% plus 30 cents per transaction for standard card payments. On a $500 invoice, that's about $14.80 in fees. On a $5,000 invoice, it's roughly $145. Factor this into your pricing if Stripe is your primary payment method.

The more significant issue is chargebacks. When a client pays by card through Stripe, they retain the ability to dispute the charge with their bank for up to 120 days from the transaction date. For services billed in advance of delivery, the window can start from the service date rather than the payment date, which can extend exposure further. In rare cases involving certain dispute reason codes, the window can stretch to 540 days. That means a payment you thought was settled can come back to haunt you over a year later.

When a chargeback is filed, Stripe immediately pulls the disputed amount from your account before the dispute is resolved. You then have 7 to 21 days, depending on the card network, to submit evidence contesting the dispute. Miss that window and you automatically lose. Stripe charges a $15 dispute fee when a chargeback is filed, win or lose. If you contest and lose, an additional $15 counter fee applies, for a total of $30 on top of the lost payment. The bank then takes 60 to 75 days to review the evidence and make a decision. The whole process typically takes two to three months and can extend longer if arbitration is involved.

Your best defense against chargebacks on Stripe is documentation. Your signed SOW, your confirmation emails, any evidence that the client received and approved the work. Stripe provides a dispute response portal where you can upload this evidence. The same records that protect you in a scope dispute protect you in a Stripe chargeback.

■ **Danger Zone:** When a chargeback is filed on Stripe, the disputed amount is pulled from your Stripe account immediately, before the dispute is resolved. This is exactly why your Stripe account should be linked to a dedicated business account, not your primary checking or savings. The funds pulled are business funds. If your Stripe chargeback rate gets too high, Stripe can place a reserve on your account, holding back a percentage of every payment for 30 or more days, or terminate your account entirely. This is why chargebacks are a business risk, not just an inconvenience. One or two disputes won't trigger this. A pattern will.

Checks and ACH Transfers

Paper checks and ACH bank transfers are still legitimate payment methods and worth accepting, particularly for established business clients and corporate accounts that have internal processes requiring them. Some clients, especially larger companies, institutions, or clients with formal accounts payable departments, will default to check or ACH regardless of what you prefer, because that's how their systems work.

Checks are slow. Expect five to seven business days from receipt to cleared funds, and build that into your cash flow planning. Don't treat a check as received payment until it clears. Mobile deposit is fine for most amounts, but very large checks, above your bank's mobile deposit limit, typically $5,000 to $10,000, may need to be deposited in person, with a hold period before funds are fully available.

ACH transfers are electronic bank-to-bank payments that typically clear in one to three business days, though some banks post them faster. They carry no transaction fee on your end, unlike card payments, and there is no chargeback mechanism equivalent to credit card disputes. ACH disputes do exist under Regulation E, but they are narrow: unauthorized transactions and processing errors. A client who authorized the transfer and later regrets it has very limited recourse through ACH. Under NACHA rules, for business-to-business ACH, the typical scenario when a corporate client pays a freelancer, the receiving bank has only two business days from settlement to return a transaction as unauthorized. After that window closes, the payment is yours. Consumer ACH has a longer 60-day window under Regulation E, but that window only covers unauthorized transactions, not authorized payments the sender later regrets. In that respect, ACH is closer to Zelle than to Stripe in terms of your protection as a recipient.

To accept ACH, you provide the client with your business bank account number and routing number. Only give these to clients you have a signed SOW with and some established trust. Unlike a card payment, which requires no access to your banking details, an ACH pull requires that the client have your account information. Use your dedicated business account, not your personal checking, for the same reason you use a dedicated account for Stripe: limit the exposure of any single account to business payment activity.

Stripe also supports ACH bank transfers natively, at a lower fee than card processing, typically 0.8% capped at $5 per transaction. If a client is set up for ACH and prefers to go through Stripe rather than sending your bank details directly, this is a clean option that keeps the transaction inside a platform you already manage.

> ★ **Pro Tip:** For clients who pay by check or ACH, state in your SOW that work begins upon receipt of cleared funds, not upon receipt of payment. A check that bounces is not payment. An ACH that is reversed is not payment. The cleared-funds language protects you from starting work against a payment that hasn't actually arrived.

Which Platform to Use When

For US clients: Zelle is the best option. No fees, instant settlement, no chargeback mechanism. If the client's bank supports it and they're comfortable with it, default to Zelle.

For international clients or clients who require card payment: Stripe works worldwide and accepts cards from virtually any country. The processing fee, roughly 2.9% plus $0.30 per transaction, should be built into your invoice amount and stated in your SOW as a line item. Quote the gross amount, not the net. If the client then chooses to pay via Zelle, remove the processing fee from the invoice. This creates a natural incentive for US clients to use Zelle, saves them money, and saves you the fee. State this explicitly in your SOW: "Invoices include a processing fee for card payments. This fee is waived for Zelle payments."

It is worth being explicit about the risk hierarchy across all payment methods. Zelle and ACH are the safest for you as a service provider. Authorized payments are essentially final once settled, with no meaningful chargeback mechanism available to a client who simply changes their mind. Checks are safe once cleared. The risk is front-loaded: a check can bounce or be stopped before clearing, but once cleared there is no reversal mechanism. Stripe carries the most exposure: a 120-day chargeback window, funds pulled immediately on dispute, and fees whether you win or lose. This hierarchy should inform your default preference for each client situation, not just your fee structure.

Regardless of platform, your protection against disputes comes from the same sources: a signed SOW or written confirmation before work begins, a clear record that deliverables were received, and a dedicated account so that disputed funds pull from your business account rather than your personal finances. The platform determines the mechanics of how a dispute gets filed. Your documentation determines whether you win it.

> ★ **Pro Tip:** Put your payment terms in your SOW. State which platform you accept, when payment is due, and that you reserve the right to stop work if payment is late. A client who knows the terms before the engagement starts is a client who has fewer grounds for a dispute after it ends.

Most freelancers think about insurance exactly once, when something goes wrong, and spend the following weeks wishing they had thought about it earlier. This chapter covers what you actually need, what you don't, and how to find the right coverage when the standard options are hard to locate.

The short version: health insurance is the most urgent priority and gets the most complicated. Professional liability (E&O) is the most overlooked and the most important for most freelancers. Equipment coverage is inexpensive and often skipped. Premises and commercial business insurance is only relevant in specific situations that most home-based freelancers will never encounter.

Health Insurance

The book covers this in the Freelancing Disadvantages chapter, but the core point bears repeating here in the context of actual planning. When you leave traditional employment, your employer-subsidized health insurance ends. What replaces it is either COBRA, continuing your existing plan at full cost, or a plan purchased through the ACA marketplace. Both are significantly more expensive than what you were paying as an employee.

COBRA keeps your existing coverage but you pay both the employee and employer portions of the premium. It's often the most expensive option but the path of least disruption, particularly if you have ongoing medical needs. It lasts 18 months federally, and some states (California's Cal-COBRA is one example) extend that period further. After COBRA runs out, or if you skip it, the ACA marketplace is the primary option for individual coverage.

Budget health insurance costs before you finalize the decision to freelance full-time. A family plan that cost you $200/month through an employer can easily run $2,000-3,000/month when you're covering it yourself. That number changes your math on what you need to earn to make the transition work.

Professional Liability (E&O) Insurance

Errors and Omissions insurance, also called professional liability insurance, covers you when a client claims your work caused them financial harm. The indemnification clause in your SOW protects you when the client provided bad information and the failure is on their side. E&O covers you when the failure could be on yours, or when a client decides to sue regardless of what the SOW says and you need a defense.

E&O is not expensive relative to the protection it provides. Depending on your field and coverage limits, annual premiums typically run between $500 and $2,000 for a solo freelancer. That cost is also a business expense. For anyone doing professional services work, writing, consulting, bookkeeping, AI implementation, HR work, legal document preparation, financial analysis, it is worth having before you have your first serious client, not after something goes wrong.

The hard part is finding it. Unlike auto or homeowner's insurance, E&O coverage is not standardized across insurers and is not uniformly available everywhere. Availability varies significantly by profession and by state. A policy designed for IT consultants is different from one designed for financial advisors, which is different from one designed for writers and content creators. The coverage terms, exclusions, and claim procedures differ meaningfully between them.

Where to start looking. Professional associations in your field are often the first place to check, as many negotiate group rates for members that are substantially lower than what you'd pay individually. If you're a writer, look at associations for freelance journalists, authors, or communications professionals. If you're in finance or bookkeeping, the relevant accounting associations often have group coverage options. If you're in technology or AI work, technology industry associations and some specialty insurers cover this work specifically.

If your profession doesn't have an obvious association, an independent insurance broker, not a captive agent who works for one company, is your best resource. A broker who works with small businesses and freelancers can shop multiple carriers and find coverage that matches your specific work. Be specific with them about what you do. "I write content for businesses" and "I ghostwrite books for executives that get published under their name" are different risk profiles and may be covered differently.

Questions to ask when evaluating a policy. Does it cover claims-made or occurrence? Claims-made policies only cover you if the policy is active when the claim is filed, even if the work was done years earlier. Occurrence policies cover any incident that happened during the policy period, even if the claim comes later. Claims-made is more common for professional liability and is fine, but understand what it means. If you stop freelancing and let the policy lapse, you may need a "tail" extension to cover work done while the policy was active. What are the exclusions? Some policies exclude intentional acts, criminal conduct, or work done for specific industries.

Make sure the exclusions don't carve out the work you actually do. What are the coverage limits? A $1M per-claim limit is standard for most freelancers. If you're doing high-stakes financial or legal adjacent work, consider whether you need more.

■ **Danger Zone:** Do not confuse E&O with general liability insurance. General liability covers bodily injury and property damage, someone slipping in your office, for example. E&O covers the professional advice and services you provide. Most freelancers need E&O. General liability is only relevant if clients come to your physical space.

Home Business Equipment Coverage

Your homeowner's or renter's insurance almost certainly does not cover equipment used for business purposes. This is a standard exclusion in residential policies. If your laptop, monitors, external drives, or other business equipment are stolen, damaged in a fire, or destroyed in a flood, your residential insurer may deny the claim on the grounds that the equipment was used commercially.

The fix is inexpensive. Most homeowner's and renter's insurers offer a home business endorsement, an add-on to your existing policy, that extends coverage to business equipment kept at your residence. The cost is typically $25-50 per year for modest coverage. If your equipment is more valuable (a professional camera setup, high-end audio recording equipment, multiple monitors), an inland marine policy covers business equipment specifically and travels with the equipment if you work from different locations.

Add up the replacement cost of your business equipment. If losing it would genuinely set you back financially, the coverage is worth having. If your setup is a laptop you could replace for $800, make your own assessment. The point is to make the decision consciously rather than discovering the exclusion when you file a claim.

Cyber Liability

If you handle client data, financial records, confidential business information, personal data of any kind, health information, you have exposure if that data is compromised. A data breach that exposes client financial records, a ransomware attack that locks you out of client files, accidental disclosure of proprietary business information, all of these create liability that standard E&O policies may not cover.

Cyber liability coverage is specifically for this. It covers the costs of notifying affected parties, credit monitoring services if personal data is involved, legal defense, and in some cases the ransom payment if you're hit with ransomware. For bookkeepers, accountants, HR consultants, AI implementers working with customer data, and anyone else who regularly handles sensitive client information, it's worth looking at alongside E&O.

Cyber liability is still a relatively new category and pricing varies widely. Some E&O policies include basic cyber coverage as part of the package. Check whether yours does before buying a separate policy. If it doesn't, standalone cyber policies start around $500-1,000 per year for solo freelancers with modest data exposure.

What You Probably Don't Need

Commercial premises insurance, covering a physical business location, client liability on premises, and related coverage, is only relevant if clients come to your physical workspace or you have employees working from a location you're responsible for. If you work from home, meet clients virtually, and have no employees, this category doesn't apply to your situation. Don't let an insurance agent sell you a commercial business policy because it sounds professional. It covers risks you don't have.

Workers' compensation covers employees. If you have no employees, you don't need it. Some states require self-employed workers to carry it in specific industries like construction, but for knowledge workers and professional services freelancers, it's not relevant.

The Right Order

If you're building your insurance coverage from scratch, here is a reasonable sequence. First, solve the health insurance problem: understand your COBRA window, research marketplace options, and make sure you have coverage before you need it. Second, get E&O in place before your first serious professional engagement. Third, check your homeowner's or renter's policy for the business equipment exclusion and add the endorsement if you need it. Fourth, evaluate cyber liability based on the sensitivity of the data you handle. Everything else is situational.

> ★ **Pro Tip:** Talk to an independent broker who specializes in small business and freelance coverage, not a generalist agent. The broker's job is to find coverage across multiple carriers. An agent who represents one company can only offer what that company sells. For E&O in particular, the difference in price and coverage terms between carriers can be significant enough to make the broker conversation worth an hour of your time.

Insurance is not optional once you're operating as a professional. It's part of what separates a freelancer who is running a business from one who is just doing gig work. The costs are manageable, the protection is real, and the downside of not having it, paying a legal defense out of pocket, losing clients because you can't demonstrate professional coverage, having an uninsured claim wipe out months of income, is far worse than the annual premium.

Making It Work with ADHD and Neurodivergence

This chapter is written specifically for people with ADHD, autism, or other forms of neurodivergence. If that's not you, the core methodology in this book works for neurotypical brains too. You can skip ahead to the next chapter. But if you've tried the standard productivity advice and felt broken by it, keep reading.

Most advice about building online income streams assumes you have a neurotypical brain. It assumes you can stick to schedules, maintain consistent focus, and power through boring tasks through sheer willpower. It assumes you can follow systems designed by and for people whose brains work predictably.

If you're ADHD, autistic, or otherwise neurodivergent, most of this advice doesn't just fail - it makes you feel broken. You try to follow the productivity systems that work for other people and wonder why you can't make yourself do simple tasks consistently. You blame yourself for lacking discipline when the real problem is that you're using tools designed for a different type of brain.

I'm ADHD and building sustainable income streams while neurodivergent requires a completely different approach. You can't force your brain to work like a neurotypical brain, but you can build systems that work with your brain's natural patterns instead of against them.

Freelancing, despite its flaws, can be much better suited to neurodivergent brains than traditional employment. The variety, the flexibility, the ability to work during your peak energy hours - these things can turn ADHD "weaknesses" into competitive advantages if you structure them correctly.

But you have to understand how your brain works and build accordingly. You can't copy neurotypical strategies and expect them to work for you.

Why Traditional Advice Fails for Different Brains

Most productivity and business advice is written by neurotypical people for neurotypical people. It assumes consistent energy levels, predictable motivation, and the ability to force yourself to do boring tasks through discipline alone.

"Just stick to a schedule." "Create a morning routine and follow it every day." "Break big tasks into smaller tasks." "Use willpower to push through resistance." This advice isn't wrong for neurotypical brains, but it's useless or counterproductive for neurodivergent brains.

ADHD brains don't have consistent energy or motivation. We have hyperfocus periods where we can work for 12 hours straight on something interesting, and we have brain fog periods where we can't make ourselves answer a simple email. We can't just decide to focus on command, and we can't force ourselves to care about things that don't interest us.

Executive dysfunction means we struggle with planning, prioritizing, and task initiation. Breaking a big task into smaller tasks doesn't help if we can't figure out which small task to do first, or if we get overwhelmed by the number of small tasks we've created.

★ **Pro Tip:** If productivity advice makes you feel worse about yourself instead of more productive, it's probably designed for a different type of brain than yours.

Traditional time management assumes you can estimate how long tasks will take and stick to schedules. ADHD brains are notoriously bad at time estimation. What seems like a 30-minute task turns into a 3-hour rabbit hole. What seems like a major project turns out to take 20 minutes once you finally start it.

The advice to "just eliminate distractions" ignores the reality that ADHD brains need stimulation to function. We often work better with background noise, multiple browser tabs open, and fidget toys nearby. What looks like distraction to neurotypical observers is often necessary stimulation for ADHD focus.

"Just push through the boring parts" assumes that willpower is a renewable resource that you can deploy on command. For ADHD brains, willpower is more like a battery that drains quickly and needs conditions to recharge. You can't just decide to have more willpower.

The result is that neurodivergent people try to follow neurotypical advice, fail repeatedly, and conclude that they're lazy, undisciplined, or not cut out for entrepreneurship. The problem isn't with you - the problem is with advice that doesn't account for how your brain works.

Using Hyperfocus Periods Productively

Hyperfocus is ADHD's superpower, but most people don't know how to use it strategically. When you're in hyperfocus, you can accomplish more in a few hours than most people accomplish in days. The key is recognizing when hyperfocus is happening and having systems in place to maximize it.

You can't schedule hyperfocus - it emerges when certain conditions align. High interest in the task, clear goals, minimal distractions, and the right level of mental stimulation. You can't force these conditions, but you can create environments where they're more likely to occur.

I do my best work during hyperfocus periods that usually happen between 10 PM and 2 AM. Traditional productivity advice says I should work during "normal" hours and get more sleep. But fighting my natural rhythm is less productive than embracing it. I schedule important work for my peak hyperfocus hours and use other times for routine tasks.

When hyperfocus kicks in, I drop everything else and ride it as long as possible. If I'm hyperfocused on writing, I'll cancel meetings and ignore emails to maximize the session. Hyperfocus periods are too valuable to waste on activities that don't require intense concentration.

> ▲ **Caution:** Don't try to force hyperfocus or feel guilty when it doesn't happen. It's a natural brain state that emerges under the right conditions, not a productivity technique you can control.

The key is having projects ready for hyperfocus when it strikes. I keep a list of high-concentration tasks that are perfect for hyperfocus periods: writing difficult articles, developing new service offerings, analyzing complex client problems. When I feel hyperfocus starting, I grab something from this list instead of wasting the session on email or administrative tasks.

I also batch similar tasks for hyperfocus periods. If I'm hyperfocused on writing, I'll write multiple articles in one session instead of trying to switch between writing and other activities. Context switching kills hyperfocus, so I protect these periods from interruption.

Not all tasks are suitable for hyperfocus. Email, scheduling, basic research, routine client communication - these tasks are better done during regular focus periods when hyperfocus would be overkill. Save hyperfocus for work that requires deep thinking and creative problem-solving.

Managing Executive Dysfunction in Gig Work

Executive dysfunction is the ADHD symptom that causes the most problems in traditional employment: difficulty with planning, prioritizing, task initiation, and working memory. In traditional jobs, these functions are often handled by managers, structured schedules, and external accountability. In gig work, you have to manage them yourself.

The solution isn't to develop better executive function (though that can help). The solution is to build external systems that handle executive function for you.

Task initiation systems. The hardest part of any task is starting it. I use implementation intentions: "When X happens, I will do Y." When I finish my morning coffee, I will open my task list. When I sit down at my desk, I will start with the easiest task. When I complete a client project, I will immediately update my invoice tracker.

These if-then rules remove the need to decide what to do next. The decision is made in advance when executive function is working, and then executed automatically when it's not.

Planning and prioritizing systems. I don't rely on my brain to remember priorities or deadlines. Everything goes into external systems: calendar appointments for deadlines, task lists with priorities clearly marked, project management tools that show what needs to happen next.

The key is making the systems simple enough that you'll use them consistently. Complex project management systems don't work if you need executive function to maintain them. I use basic tools: a calendar, a simple task list, and file folders organized by client and project.

> ■ **Danger Zone:** Don't create planning systems that require more executive function to maintain than they provide. Simple systems that you use are better than complex systems that you abandon.

Working memory supports. ADHD brains have limited working memory, which makes it hard to hold multiple pieces of information in mind while working on complex tasks. I externalize working memory by writing everything down: meeting notes, project requirements, random ideas, things I need to remember to do later.

I also use templates and checklists for recurring tasks. Client onboarding, project delivery, invoice creation - anything I do regularly gets a template so I don't have to remember all the steps each time.

Accountability systems. External accountability works better than internal motivation for ADHD brains. I schedule check-ins with clients, join coworking sessions with other freelancers, and use body doubling (working virtually "alongside" others) for tasks I'm avoiding.

Public commitments work too. Telling clients when projects will be delivered creates external deadlines that motivate action better than internal goals. Posting about projects on social media creates social accountability for completion.

Finding Income Streams That Work WITH Your Brain, Not Against It

Not all income streams are equally suited to neurodivergent brains. Some require consistent daily effort that's hard to maintain with variable energy and motivation. Others require extensive planning and organization that's challenging with executive dysfunction. Others are so repetitive that they become unbearable for brains that crave variety and stimulation.

The key is choosing income streams that align with your brain's natural patterns instead of fighting against them.

Project-based work over routine work. ADHD brains do better with projects that have clear beginnings, middles, and ends than with ongoing routine tasks. Ghostwriting a white paper is perfect for hyperfocus. Managing a client's social media accounts day after day is torture.

Each ghostwriting project is different: different client, different topic, different challenges to solve. The variety keeps my brain engaged in ways that routine work doesn't. I can hyperfocus on interesting projects and coast through easier ones when my energy is low.

Interest-driven work over obligation-driven work. ADHD brains have an interest-based nervous system. We can focus intensely on things that interest us and struggle to focus on things that don't, regardless of their importance. Fighting this pattern is exhausting and usually unsuccessful.

Instead of forcing myself to work on boring but "important" tasks, I structure my business around things I find genuinely interesting. I write about topics I want to learn about. I work with clients whose businesses fascinate me. I develop services around problems I enjoy solving.

★ **Pro Tip:** ADHD brains can often hyperfocus on "play" activities for hours while struggling to focus on "work" activities for minutes. The solution is to make your work more like play.

Flexible deadlines over rigid schedules. ADHD energy and motivation are unpredictable. Some days I can work for 12 hours and produce amazing results. Other days I can barely answer emails. Rigid daily schedules that require consistent output don't work for this reality.

I negotiate flexible deadlines with clients that allow for variable productivity. Instead of promising daily deliverables, I promise weekly or monthly deliverables. This gives me room to work intensively when energy is high and rest when energy is low.

High-stimulation work over low-stimulation work. ADHD brains need stimulation to focus. Boring, repetitive tasks don't provide enough stimulation to maintain attention. Complex, challenging tasks provide the stimulation needed for sustained focus.

I seek out complex ghostwriting projects that require research, analysis, and creative problem-solving. Simple blog posts about obvious topics bore me to tears. In-depth white papers about emerging technologies can hold my attention for hours.

The Advantages of Neurodivergent Thinking in Finding Niches

While ADHD creates challenges in traditional employment, it also creates advantages in entrepreneurship and niche-finding that neurotypical brains often miss.

Pattern recognition. ADHD brains are excellent at noticing patterns and connections that others miss. We see relationships between seemingly unrelated things. We spot trends before they become obvious. We identify opportunities in the gaps between established categories.

I found the ghostwriting niche partly because my brain made connections that other writers didn't see. I noticed that executives were asking for content but didn't want attribution. I saw the pattern across multiple clients before it was obvious. My brain connected "business leaders need content" with "business leaders don't have time to write" and created a service offering around that gap.

Hyperfocus intensity. When ADHD brains are interested in something, we can research it more thoroughly and think about it more deeply than neurotypical brains typically do. We become temporary experts in whatever captures our attention.

This hyperfocus learning allows us to quickly develop expertise in new niches. While others are skimming the surface of trending topics, we can dive deep enough to understand the real problems and opportunities. We can spot niches that others overlook because they didn't spend enough time exploring them.

> ▲ **Caution:** Hyperfocus learning can lead to pursuing too many interests simultaneously. Focus your deep dives on areas with real income potential, not just intellectual curiosity.

Tolerance for uncertainty. ADHD brains are used to dealing with unpredictability. Our energy, motivation, and focus are variable, so we're comfortable with situations that change frequently. This tolerance for uncertainty is valuable in this work, where market conditions shift rapidly.

While neurotypical entrepreneurs might stick with proven strategies too long, ADHD entrepreneurs are more willing to pivot when circumstances change. We're used to adapting our approach based on what's working in the moment instead of following rigid long-term plans.

Creative problem-solving. ADHD brains approach problems from unusual angles. We don't follow conventional wisdom or established procedures. We improvise solutions that others wouldn't think of. This creativity is valuable for finding market opportunities that conventional approaches miss.

When traditional marketing methods weren't working for my ghostwriting business, I tried unconventional approaches: commenting thoughtfully on executives' LinkedIn posts, writing analysis pieces about their industries, offering to interview them for "research" that turned into sales conversations. These approaches worked because they didn't feel like sales to the prospects.

Systems and Tools for Inconsistent Energy and Attention

Managing a business with ADHD requires different tools and systems than managing a business with a neurotypical brain. The key is accepting that your energy and attention will be inconsistent and building systems that work with this reality.

Energy-based scheduling instead of time-based scheduling. I don't schedule tasks based on when I "should" do them. I schedule tasks based on the type of energy they require and when I typically have that energy available.

High-concentration work gets scheduled for my peak focus hours (usually late evening). Administrative tasks get scheduled for medium-energy periods (usually mid-morning). Routine communication gets scheduled for low-energy periods (usually mid-afternoon when my brain is tired but I can still respond to emails).

Task lists organized by energy level, not priority. Traditional productivity advice says to organize tasks by importance or urgency. ADHD brains work better with tasks organized by the type of mental energy they require.

I have three categories: high-focus tasks (writing, complex problem-solving), medium-focus tasks (research, planning), and low-focus tasks (email, scheduling, administrative work). When I sit down to work, I check my energy level and choose from the appropriate category.

Multiple projects in different stages. Having only one project means that when you get stuck or lose interest, you have nowhere to go. Having multiple projects in different stages means you can switch between them based on your current energy and interest level.

I typically have 3-4 writing projects at different stages: one in research phase, one in first draft, one in revision, one in final editing. When I get stuck on one, I can switch to another without losing productivity.

> ■ **Danger Zone:** Too many simultaneous projects can become overwhelming. Find the sweet spot between having options and having chaos.

External accountability partners. ADHD brains respond better to external accountability than internal motivation. I have regular check-ins with other freelancers, participate in online coworking sessions, and schedule progress reports with clients.

Body doubling works well for ADHD brains. Working "alongside" others (even virtually) provides just enough social pressure and stimulation to maintain focus on tasks that would be impossible to do alone.

Tools that reduce friction. The easier something is to do, the more likely an ADHD brain is to do it. I use tools that minimize the steps between intention and action: text expanders for common emails, templates for recurring tasks, automated invoicing systems, cloud storage that syncs across all devices.

The goal is to reduce the number of decisions and steps required to complete routine tasks. Every extra click or decision point is an opportunity for an ADHD brain to get distracted or give up.

Why This Work Can Be Better Than Traditional Employment

Traditional employment is designed around neurotypical brains and neurotypical productivity patterns. Freelancing can be much better suited to neurodivergent brains if you structure it correctly.

Variety over monotony. Traditional jobs require doing similar tasks day after day, often for years. ADHD brains crave novelty and stimulation. Freelancing allows you to work on different projects with different clients, solving different problems each time.

Each ghostwriting project I take on is different. Different industry, different challenges, different research required. The variety keeps my brain engaged in ways that a traditional writing job never could. I'd be bored to tears writing about the same topics for the same company every day.

Natural rhythms over imposed schedules. Traditional employment requires showing up at times and working hours regardless of your natural energy patterns. This work lets you work when your brain is most productive.

I do my best work between 10 PM and 2 AM. Traditional employers would never accommodate this schedule, but my clients don't care when I do the work as long as it's delivered on time and meets their requirements.

> ★ **Pro Tip:** One of the biggest advantages of gig work for ADHD brains is the ability to work during your natural peak performance hours instead of fighting your circadian rhythms.

Interest-based selection over assigned tasks. In traditional employment, you're assigned tasks regardless of whether they interest you. In freelancing, you can choose projects that align with your interests and turn down projects that don't.

I only take on ghostwriting projects that genuinely interest me. If a potential client's business bores me, I refer them to other writers. This selectivity means I'm almost always working on something that can hold my attention and trigger hyperfocus.

Immediate feedback over delayed reviews. ADHD brains need frequent feedback to stay motivated and on track. Traditional employment often provides feedback only during quarterly or annual reviews. The gig economy provides immediate feedback through client responses, project completion, and payment.

When I finish a ghostwriting project and the client loves it, I get immediate positive reinforcement that motivates the next project. When a client requests revisions, I get immediate feedback about what needs improvement. This feedback loop is much more effective for ADHD motivation than waiting months for a performance review.

Control over environment. Traditional offices are often designed for neurotypical productivity: quiet, minimal stimulation, standardized workspaces. ADHD brains often need different environmental conditions to focus effectively.

I work with background music, multiple monitors, fidget toys, and frequent position changes. I take walking meetings and work from different locations throughout the day. I control my lighting, temperature, and noise levels. These environmental modifications would be impossible in most traditional workplaces.

Multiple Streams for ADHD Brains: Variety Over Monotony

The multiple income streams approach that's good risk management for everyone is important for ADHD brains because it provides the variety and stimulation we need to stay engaged long-term.

Having only one income stream, even a successful one, can become boring and unstimulating for an ADHD brain. What starts as exciting work can become routine drudgery once the novelty wears off. Multiple streams provide variety that keeps work interesting.

Different types of work for different brain states. Some days my brain wants to dive deep into complex research. Other days it wants to have conversations with people. Other days it wants to edit and polish existing work. Having multiple income streams means I can match my work to my current brain state.

When I'm in a social mood, I do client calls and networking. When I'm in a hyperfocus mood, I write. When I'm in a detail-oriented mood, I edit and proofread. Having options means I'm always working on something that fits my current mental energy.

Projects at different stages. ADHD brains can get stuck on parts of projects while being excited about other parts. Having multiple projects at different stages means you can always find something that matches your current interest and energy level.

I love the research phase of writing projects but sometimes struggle with first drafts. I love editing and polishing but sometimes struggle with the initial structure. Having multiple projects means I can work on research for one project while editing another and outlining a third.

> ▲ **Caution:** Don't use multiple projects as an excuse to avoid difficult tasks entirely. Sometimes you have to push through resistance, but you can choose when to fight those battles.

Short-term and long-term projects. ADHD brains often struggle with long-term projects that don't provide regular dopamine hits from completion. Mixing short-term projects (that provide frequent completion satisfaction) with long-term projects (that provide deeper engagement) creates a sustainable balance.

My ghostwriting projects typically take 2-4 weeks, providing regular completion satisfaction. My books take 3-6 months, providing deeper engagement with topics I care about. The combination prevents both boredom (from only short projects) and frustration (from only long projects).

Active and passive income streams. ADHD brains need stimulation and engagement, but we also have periods of low energy when active work is difficult. Having both active income streams (that require ongoing effort) and passive income streams (that generate money without daily attention) provides income during both high-energy and low-energy periods.

My ghostwriting requires active engagement with clients and projects. My book royalties provide passive income during periods when client work is slow or when my energy is too low for intensive work. The combination provides financial stability regardless of my current brain state.

The key is building a portfolio of income streams that collectively provide the variety, stimulation, and flexibility that ADHD brains need while still generating sustainable income. It's not about working more - it's about working in ways that align with how your brain functions instead of fighting against it.

Your ADHD is not an obstacle to overcome in building income streams. It's a different operating system that requires different strategies. Once you understand how your brain works and build accordingly, you can create income streams that are not only sustainable but more successful because they use your neurodivergent strengths instead of fighting your neurodivergent challenges.

Outsourcing: When to Delegate and When You're Just Being Lazy

The internet is full of entrepreneurs bragging about their teams of virtual assistants who handle everything while they sip cocktails on beaches. "I hired a VA for $5/hour and now I work 10 hours a week!" "My Filipino team runs my entire business!" "Outsource everything and scale to six figures!"

Most of this is fantasy designed to sell courses about building virtual teams. The reality of outsourcing is messier, more expensive, and more time-consuming than the marketers want you to believe.

I've tried outsourcing many times with mixed results. Some experiments saved me time and money. Others cost more in management overhead than they saved in labor costs. Many turned into expensive lessons about why some work should never be delegated.

The key to successful outsourcing isn't finding the cheapest labor possible. It's understanding what can be delegated effectively, what the true costs are, and when your time is better spent doing the work yourself instead of managing someone else doing it poorly.

Outsourcing can be a powerful tool for scaling your business, but only if you approach it strategically instead of treating it as a magic solution to working less.

The Outsourcing Fantasy vs. Reality

The outsourcing fantasy goes like this: identify repetitive tasks in your business, hire cheap virtual assistants to handle them, and suddenly you have more time to focus on high-value work while your costs go down and your profits go up.

The reality is that outsourcing often increases your workload in the short term and sometimes permanently. You have to create detailed instructions, train new people, review their work, handle miscommunications, and manage the relationship ongoing. Many entrepreneurs spend more time managing outsourced work than they would have spent doing the work themselves.

"Replace yourself with $5/hour VAs" advice ignores the hidden costs of delegation. The time you spend writing job postings, screening candidates, training new hires, reviewing work, handling revisions, and managing ongoing relationships isn't free. When you factor in these costs, cheap labor becomes expensive very quickly.

> ■ **Danger Zone:** If you're paying someone $5/hour to do work that takes you 30 minutes, but you spend 2 hours managing them, you're not saving money - you're buying yourself a low-paying management job.

I hired a VA to handle email management and calendar scheduling. The hourly rate was low, but training her took 8 hours, creating standard operating procedures took 4 hours, and ongoing communication took 30 minutes per day. After three months, I calculated that I was effectively paying $25/hour for work that saved me $15/hour of my own time.

The hidden costs of managing outsourced work include communication overhead, quality control, revision rounds, and the opportunity cost of time spent on management instead of revenue-generating activities. These costs are real but rarely discussed in outsourcing success stories.

When outsourcing makes sense: when you have clearly defined, repeatable processes that someone else can execute without constant supervision, when the work doesn't require your specific expertise or judgment, and when you have more high-value work than you can handle personally.

When outsourcing is just ego: when you want to feel like a "real entrepreneur" with a team, when you're trying to avoid work you find boring but not expensive, or when you're scaling for the sake of scaling rather than to solve actual bottlenecks.

> ★ **Pro Tip:** Before outsourcing any task, document the process completely enough that you could train a replacement in 30 minutes. If you can't create clear procedures, the task isn't ready for delegation.

Virtual Assistants: The Good, Bad, and Expensive

Virtual assistants can be valuable for administrative tasks that don't require specialized knowledge but do require significant time investment. They're terrible for anything that requires judgment, creativity, or deep understanding of your business.

What VAs can do well: data entry, appointment scheduling, email filtering, basic research, simple content formatting, social media posting from provided content, and other clearly defined administrative tasks with measurable outcomes.

What VAs can't do well: anything that requires understanding context, making judgment calls, representing your brand voice, handling sensitive client communications, or solving problems that don't have clear procedures.

I use a VA for formatting completed articles for publication. These tasks have clear specifications and measurable outcomes. The VA doesn't need to understand the content or make creative decisions. Just follow detailed procedures.

But I tried using VAs for client communication and project management, and it was a disaster. They couldn't understand the nuances of client relationships, made decisions that created problems, and required constant supervision for tasks that demanded business judgment.

Finding reliable VAs without getting scammed requires looking beyond price and focusing on communication skills, reliability, and portfolio quality. The cheapest VAs are usually cheap for good reasons - poor English skills, unreliable internet, or lack of relevant experience.

> ▲ **Caution:** VAs who promise they can handle "anything" are usually good at nothing. Look for specialists in specific tasks rather than generalists who claim universal competence.

The real cost of "cheap" overseas labor includes time zone coordination challenges, communication delays, cultural misunderstandings, and higher turnover rates. An $8/hour VA who delivers reliable work is cheaper than a $3/hour VA who requires constant management and produces inconsistent results.

Managing VA relationships for results requires clear expectations, detailed procedures, regular check-ins, and performance metrics. Treat VAs like remote employees, not like magic solutions that require no management.

I pay my current VA \$12/hour, which is higher than many overseas rates but lower than US rates. She's reliable, communicates clearly, and requires minimal supervision. The premium over bottom-market rates is worth it for the reduced management overhead.

Fiverr and the Race to the Bottom

Fiverr has created a marketplace where the lowest price often wins, regardless of quality. This race to the bottom benefits buyers looking for cheap work but hurts service providers trying to make sustainable livings.

Why most Fiverr work is garbage: providers compete primarily on price, leading to cut corners, rushed deliveries, and minimal communication. The \$5 logo design is created from templates in 10 minutes. The \$10 article is spun from existing content or generated by AI.

When Fiverr work isn't garbage: when you find providers who've built strong reputations and charge accordingly, when you're buying simple, clearly defined services where quality is easy to measure, or when you need quick, disposable work for testing purposes.

I've used Fiverr successfully for simple graphic design tasks like social media headers and basic logos for testing purposes. For \$15-25, I can get decent graphics that would take me hours to create myself. But I wouldn't use Fiverr for important branding or client-facing materials.

The platform dependency trap affects both buyers and sellers on Fiverr. Sellers build their businesses on a platform they don't control, risking account suspension or policy changes. Buyers become dependent on specific sellers without direct contact information or alternative ways to work together.

Finding diamonds in the rough requires looking at portfolios carefully, reading reviews for specific feedback about communication and revisions, and starting with small test projects before committing to larger work.

Price vs. quality on Fiverr follows predictable patterns. Services under $10 are usually template-based or AI-generated. Services in the $25-100 range often provide decent value for simple tasks. Services over $100 might be worth paying, but at that price point, you should consider alternatives to Fiverr.

> ■ **Danger Zone:** Don't use Fiverr for anything mission-critical to your business. The savings aren't worth the risk of poor quality or missed deadlines.

The platform takes a significant cut from both buyers and sellers, making it expensive for ongoing relationships. If you find a good provider on Fiverr, consider moving the relationship off-platform for future work.

International vs. Same-Country Outsourcing

Time zone realities create more problems than most people anticipate. When your VA is 12 hours ahead or behind, urgent issues become next-day problems. Real-time collaboration becomes impossible. Simple questions turn into email threads that take days to resolve.

I worked with a VA in the Philippines who was excellent at her job, but the 12-hour time difference made collaboration difficult. When I needed quick changes for client deadlines, I had to wait until the next day for responses. The time zone difference ultimately made the relationship unsustainable despite her quality work.

Language and cultural barriers cost more than they save when they lead to misunderstandings, missed nuances, or work that doesn't match your expectations. "Native-level English" often means "good enough for basic communication" but not good enough for representing your business professionally.

Cultural differences in communication styles can create problems. Some cultures are more direct, others more indirect. Some prioritize speed, others prioritize avoiding mistakes. These differences aren't right or wrong, but they can cause friction in working relationships.

When local costs are worth paying: for anything client-facing, for work that requires cultural understanding, for tasks that need real-time collaboration, or when the quality difference justifies the price difference.

I pay US-based contractors for client communication, content editing, and anything that represents my business directly. The higher hourly rates are worth it for better communication, cultural understanding, and time zone alignment.

Legal and tax implications of international contractors vary by country but often include withholding requirements, reporting obligations, and potential classification issues. Consult with an accountant about your specific situation, especially if you're paying significant amounts to international contractors.

> ★ **Pro Tip:** For international contractors, use payment platforms that handle tax reporting and provide proper documentation. PayPal, Wise, and similar services create audit trails that cash payments don't.

What to Outsource vs. What to Keep In-House

Core competencies you should never outsource are the skills and knowledge that make your business valuable. For a ghostwriter, that's client interviewing and content creation. For a consultant, that's strategy development and client relationships. For a designer, that's creative direction and client communication.

Outsourcing core competencies might save money short-term, but it prevents you from building expertise and relationships that create long-term value. You become a middleman in your own business instead of a value creator.

Administrative tasks worth delegating: data entry, appointment scheduling, basic research, file organization, email filtering, social media posting, transcription, and other clearly defined tasks that don't require specialized knowledge.

I handle transcription through AI tools rather than a VA because the tools are faster and more accurate for my purposes. I don't outsource client interviews because the relationship building and content extraction are core to my value proposition.

The handoff problem occurs when the effort required to delegate work exceeds the effort required to do the work yourself. This happens when tasks are complex, poorly defined, or require too much context to explain effectively.

If it takes longer to explain a task than to do it yourself, delegation doesn't make sense. If the task requires constant back-and-forth communication, delegation creates more work than it eliminates.

To make outsourcing possible, document procedures, create templates, establish quality standards, and develop training materials. This upfront investment is only worthwhile if you'll be delegating the same type of work repeatedly.

Red Flags and How to Avoid Getting Burned

Spotting fake portfolios and inflated reviews requires looking for specific details rather than general praise. Real client work has specifics about challenges, solutions, and results. Fake portfolios use generic descriptions and stock imagery.

Check whether portfolio samples match the provider's claimed expertise. A logo designer whose portfolio includes only simple text-based logos might not be capable of complex brand design. A writer whose samples are all short blog posts might struggle with long-form content.

Communication red flags that predict problems: unclear responses to direct questions, promises that seem too good to be true, reluctance to discuss specifics about process or timeline, and poor grammar or unclear English in initial communications.

If someone can't communicate clearly during the sales process, they probably can't communicate clearly during the work process. If they make unrealistic promises to win your business, they'll probably make excuses when they can't deliver.

Payment scams and how to protect yourself: never pay large amounts upfront, use payment platforms that offer buyer protection, start with small test projects before committing to larger work, and be suspicious of providers who insist on wire transfers or cryptocurrency payments.

> ▲ **Caution:** Any provider who demands full payment upfront or refuses to use standard payment platforms is probably running a scam.

When to cut losses and find someone else: when communication becomes difficult, when deadlines are missed repeatedly, when quality doesn't improve after feedback, or when you're spending more time managing the relationship than the work is worth.

I have a three-strike rule for outsourced work. First missed deadline or quality issue gets a conversation about expectations. Second issue gets a formal warning and process adjustment. Third issue ends the relationship immediately.

Don't fall for the sunk cost fallacy with bad contractors. The time and money you've already invested is gone regardless. The question is whether continuing the relationship will be productive going forward.

The Economics of Delegation

Calculating the true cost of outsourced work requires including all hidden costs: time spent finding contractors, training them, managing ongoing work, handling revisions, and dealing with problems.

A $10/hour VA who requires 2 hours of management per week costs $10/hour plus your hourly rate times 2. If your time is worth $50/hour, that "cheap" VA effectively costs $110/hour for 8 hours of work.

When your time is worth more than the savings, delegation makes financial sense even if the hourly rate is higher than overseas alternatives. A $25/hour US-based contractor who requires minimal management might be cheaper than an $8/hour overseas contractor who requires constant supervision.

Hidden costs include revision rounds, project management, quality control, communication overhead, and the opportunity cost of time spent on delegation instead of revenue-generating work.

I track the total time I spend on outsourced projects, including finding contractors, training, ongoing management, and quality control. Many projects that looked like money-savers turned out to cost more than doing the work myself once I included all time investments.

Long-term relationships vs. one-off projects changes the economics significantly. The upfront costs of finding and training good contractors are amortized over many projects. One-off projects rarely justify the investment in finding quality providers.

> ★ **Pro Tip:** Calculate your effective hourly rate for outsourced work by dividing your total time investment (including management) by the hours of work you received. Many "cheap" arrangements are expensive when you do the math.

My best outsourcing relationships have lasted for years. The initial investment in finding and training was high, but the ongoing value has been significant because the contractors understand my expectations and require minimal management.

Alternatives to Traditional Outsourcing

Automation tools vs. human delegation often provide better value for routine tasks. Email filters, scheduling software, and content management systems can handle many administrative tasks without the management overhead of human contractors.

I use automation for email sorting, social media scheduling, invoice generation, and file backup. These tools require initial setup time but minimal ongoing management. They're more reliable than humans for simple, repetitive tasks.

Profit-sharing arrangements instead of hourly rates align incentives better for outcome-focused work. Instead of paying someone to write articles, pay them based on traffic or engagement generated. Instead of paying for social media management, pay based on follower growth or engagement metrics.

These arrangements work when outcomes are measurable and the contractor has control over results. They don't work for tasks where outcomes depend on factors outside the contractor's control.

Collaborative partnerships vs. traditional contractor relationships create better alignment for ongoing work. Instead of hiring someone to do tasks you don't want to do, partner with someone whose skills complement yours for mutual benefit.

I have referral partnerships with other writers where we share overflow work and client referrals. This creates value for both parties without the management overhead of traditional outsourcing.

When doing it yourself is still the best option: for core business activities, for work that requires your specific expertise, for tasks that change frequently, or when the management overhead exceeds the time savings.

> ■ **Danger Zone:** Don't outsource just because you can. Outsource when it creates clear financial benefits after accounting for all costs and risks.

The goal of outsourcing should be to free up your time for higher-value work, not to avoid work you find boring. If outsourcing doesn't enable you to earn more money or create more value, it's probably not worth the complexity.

Successful outsourcing requires clear objectives, realistic expectations, proper systems, and ongoing management. It's a business tool, not a shortcut to working less.

When done right, outsourcing can scale your business and increase your income. When done wrong, it creates expensive headaches that cost more than they save.

Conclusion: Find Your Own Path

If you've made it this far, you've probably noticed that this book doesn't end with a step-by-step blueprint for guaranteed success. There's no "follow these 10 steps and make $10,000 next month" promise. No affiliate links to courses that will supposedly teach you everything I left out.

That's intentional.

The biggest lie in this space is that there's a one-size-fits-all formula for success. That you can copy someone else's exact methods and get the same results. That success comes from following instructions rather than developing judgment.

This lie is profitable for course creators and platform owners, but it's destructive for the people who believe it. They waste time and money chasing other people's successes instead of building their own. They blame themselves when cookie-cutter strategies don't work in their unique situations. They give up when they should be experimenting.

Your path to sustainable income will be different from mine. Different from the case studies in this book. Different from whatever guru is currently promising easy money on YouTube. It has to be different because your skills, circumstances, constraints, and goals are different.

But the principles for finding that path are universal. The experimentation methodology works regardless of what you're testing. The framework for evaluating opportunities applies whether you're considering ghostwriting, e-commerce, or something that doesn't exist yet. The reality check process helps you avoid common mistakes regardless of which specific mistakes you might be tempted to make.

Every success story is the edited highlight reel of someone's path, skills, timing, and market conditions that made it work for them in their specific moment. The antidote isn't finding a better story to copy. It's the Experimentation Method in Part II: your own inventory, your own riskiest assumption, your own test. If you skipped that chapter, go back. If you read it, you already have what you need.

Building Multiple Streams That Fit YOUR Brain and Skills

The multiple income streams approach isn't about having as many streams as possible. It's about having the right combination of streams for your skills, interests, constraints, and goals.

Your optimal portfolio depends on factors that are unique to you: your risk tolerance, available time, existing skills, learning preferences, financial needs, and life circumstances. Someone with young children needs different income streams than someone who can travel freely. Someone with ADHD needs different approaches than someone with neurotypical focus patterns.

Build on your existing strengths instead of trying to develop entirely new competencies. If you're good with people, look for opportunities that involve communication and relationship building. If you're good with systems, look for opportunities that involve process optimization and automation.

I built my income streams around writing skills I already had rather than trying to learn completely new fields like coding or design. This let me achieve profitability faster and with less risk than starting from scratch in unfamiliar areas.

But don't limit yourself to obvious applications of your skills. Look for unexpected ways to use your knowledge and abilities. The most profitable opportunities are often in the intersections between different fields or in applications that others haven't considered.

Consider your natural work patterns and energy cycles. If you're most productive early in the morning, choose income streams that let you work during peak hours. If you prefer project-based work to ongoing commitments, structure your services accordingly.

> ★ **Pro Tip:** Your weird combination of skills, interests, and constraints is an advantage. It helps you see opportunities that people with more conventional backgrounds miss.

Think about sustainability over time. Can you do this work for years without burning out? Does it build skills and relationships that become more valuable with experience? Will you still find it interesting after the novelty wears off?

Don't just optimize for maximum short-term income. Optimize for the combination of income, sustainability, skill development, and personal satisfaction that works for your specific situation and goals.

The Importance of Ethics and Sustainability

Building income streams that depend on taking advantage of people or providing minimal value might work short-term, but it's not sustainable long-term.

Unethical business practices eventually catch up with you through reputation damage, customer churn, or regulatory problems.

More importantly, building something you can't be proud of creates psychological costs that outweigh financial benefits. If you have to hide what you do for work or make excuses for your business practices, you're probably not building something sustainable.

The ethics test is simple: Can you explain your business to your family and friends without embarrassment? Would you be comfortable if your practices were featured in a news article? Could you recommend your services to people you care about?

I've turned down profitable opportunities because they didn't pass the ethics test. Promoting products I hadn't used, targeting vulnerable populations, or making claims I couldn't substantiate. These decisions cost money short-term but protected my reputation and self-respect long-term.

Sustainability also means building practices that you can maintain without destroying your health, relationships, or mental well-being. Hustle culture promises that sacrifice today leads to freedom tomorrow, but sustainable success requires balance throughout the process.

Don't build income streams that require working 80-hour weeks, constantly chasing new clients, or living in constant stress about money. These approaches might generate income temporarily, but they're not sustainable for most people over years or decades.

> ■ **Danger Zone:** Any business model that requires you to constantly find new customers because you can't keep existing ones is fundamentally broken.

Focus on creating genuine value for customers rather than extracting maximum value from them. Businesses that help customers achieve their goals create loyal relationships that provide stability and growth opportunities. Businesses that exploit customers create adversarial relationships that require constant customer replacement.

Think about the long-term impact of your work on yourself, your customers, and your industry. Are you making things better or just making money? Are you solving real problems or creating artificial ones? Are you building something that improves with time or something that gets harder to sustain?

Final Thoughts on Cutting Through the Noise

This space is full of noise. Platforms promising easy money. Influencers selling courses about their success. News articles alternating between "gig work is liberation" and "gig work is exploitation." Everyone has opinions about what you should do and how you should do it.

Most of this noise is designed to benefit the people creating it, not the people consuming it. Platforms want users who will generate transaction fees. Course creators want customers who will buy their products. Media outlets want stories that generate clicks and engagement.

Your job is to filter this noise and focus on what matters for your specific situation. Not what's trending on social media. Not what worked for someone else last year. Not what platforms are promoting this month. What works for you, with your skills and constraints, in current market conditions.

This requires developing judgment rather than following instructions. Instructions become obsolete when conditions change. Judgment helps you adapt to new situations and identify opportunities that others miss.

The principles in this book aren't going to become obsolete because they're based on human psychology and market dynamics that don't change quickly. People will always have problems they're willing to pay to solve. Markets will always reward value creation and punish value extraction. Quality work will always command higher prices than commodity work.

But the specific tactics and opportunities will continue evolving. New platforms will emerge and existing ones will change. New technologies will create opportunities and eliminate others. Economic conditions will shift demand from some services to others.

Your ability to adapt and experiment will determine your long-term success more than your ability to execute any specific strategy perfectly. Stay curious, test new ideas, measure results honestly, and build on what works while abandoning what doesn't.

The goal isn't to find the perfect opportunity that will work forever. It's to develop the skills and systems for continuously finding opportunities that work for your current situation.

Don't wait for perfect information or ideal conditions before you start. Don't let fear of failure prevent you from testing ideas. Don't let other people's success stories make you feel inadequate about your own progress.

Start with what you have, where you are, with the skills you currently possess. Test small, learn fast, and build on what works. Your path won't look like anyone else's path, and that's exactly how it should be.

Real opportunities exist for people who approach this strategically rather than desperately. For people who focus on creating value rather than chasing money. For people who build systems rather than just completing tasks.

You don't need permission from anyone to start building income streams. You don't need perfect plans or guaranteed outcomes. You just need the willingness to experiment, the discipline to measure results honestly, and the judgment to adapt when conditions change.

Your path is waiting for you to create it.

Your First 30 Days

This isn't a blueprint. It's an application of the experimentation method to your first month, a way to start moving without requiring perfect information or significant investment.

Spend the first week on the inventory. Write down everything you know how to do, not just professionally, but personally. Skills you use at work, skills you use at home, things people routinely ask you for help with. Then go through the list and mark anything where you know people have paid money for that skill or knowledge. Don't filter for what seems scalable or impressive. Just be honest about what you can actually do that others find difficult.

In the second week, pick two or three candidates from that list and talk to five real people about each one. Not a survey, not a Reddit post, but actual conversations with people who might hire you or who know people who would. You're not pitching yet. You're trying to find out if the problem you solve is real, how often it comes up, and what people currently do about it. Listen for frustration. Frustration means unmet demand.

In the third week, design one test around the most promising candidate. Keep it small enough that failing costs you less than a week of effort. Write down what success looks like before you run it, a specific outcome, not a feeling. If your test involves offering a service, charge for it from day one, even if the rate is low. Free work validates nothing. Paid work validates demand.

In the fourth week, evaluate against what you wrote down in week three, not against how you feel about it. If it cleared the bar, figure out how to do it again and do it better. If it didn't, write down what you learned and pick the next candidate. Either result is useful. The only failure is spending 30 days reading about starting instead of starting.

Thirty days from now you'll either have early evidence of something worth pursuing, a clear reason to try something else, or both. That's more useful than six more months of research.

About the Author

I'm not a business guru, motivational speaker, or someone who got rich selling courses about getting rich. I'm a freelance ghostwriter and book coach who stumbled into a sustainable income after years of trying strategies that didn't work.

My path to freelancing wasn't inspirational. I was burned out from traditional employment, tired of office politics, and convinced that trading time for money on someone else's schedule was slowly killing my soul. I have ADHD, which made the rigid structure and arbitrary deadlines of corporate life particularly miserable.

I started exploring online income opportunities out of desperation, not ambition. I tried affiliate marketing, dropshipping, online surveys, content mills, and various platform-based work. Most of these experiments failed spectacularly. I wasted money on courses that promised easy success and spent countless hours implementing strategies that generated minimal income.

The breakthrough came when I stopped trying to copy other people's success stories and started paying attention to what my existing clients were asking for. Several business owners wanted content written under their names rather than mine. This led to ghostwriting, which turned out to be a perfect fit for my skills and working style.

I've been ghostwriting for business executives and consultants for over twelve years. I've also published several books under my own name, built a small but profitable editing business, and developed systems that let me work from anywhere with a decent internet connection.

My total income from these streams has grown from $500 in my first month to consistently over $10,000 per month, with peak months reaching $15,000. These aren't get-rich-quick numbers, but they represent financial independence that would have been impossible in traditional employment given my constraints and preferences.

What those numbers don't show: I left employment before I started experimenting, not after. I had savings, which bought me time: eighteen months of COBRA coverage followed by eighteen more months of Cal-COBRA, which meant health insurance wasn't the crisis it is for people who leave without a cushion. That runway matters. The methodology in this book is designed to work without it, but I'd be lying if I said having it didn't change what risks I could take and how long I could wait for things to work. If you have runway, use it deliberately. If you don't, the survival and bridge work framework is the substitute.

More importantly, I've built something sustainable that works with my brain rather than against it. I can hyperfocus on interesting projects during my peak hours, take time off when I need it, and choose clients whose work genuinely interests me. I haven't had a boss or attended a mandatory meeting in twelve years.

I'm not sharing this to brag about my success or to suggest that everyone should follow my exact path. I'm sharing it because I spent years consuming advice from people whose main business was selling advice, and I want to offer a different perspective from someone whose main business is doing the work.

This book grew out of conversations with friends and family members who were interested in building alternative income streams but overwhelmed by conflicting advice and unrealistic promises. I realized that the methodology I'd developed for finding and testing opportunities might be useful to people facing similar challenges.

I write about business and productivity topics on my blog and contribute to various publications in the entrepreneurship space. But my primary focus remains client work, not teaching or content creation. I believe the best business advice comes from people who are currently doing the work, not from people who did it briefly and then moved on to teaching about it.

I live in Clearwater, Florida, work from a simple home office setup, and spend my free time hiking, painting fantasy miniatures, and building plastic model kits. I'm not traveling the world or living in a mansion, but I have the flexibility to structure my work around my life instead of the other way around.

If you're looking for inspiration or motivation, there are better sources. If you're looking for practical methodology from someone who's built sustainable income streams without venture capital, trust funds, or unique advantages, this book might be helpful.

The strategies and principles I share have worked for me and for others I know who've applied them systematically. But they require work, patience, and the willingness to experiment with ideas that might not pan out. There are no shortcuts or guarantees, just frameworks for making better decisions and avoiding common mistakes.

I'm still learning and adapting as market conditions change. The gig economy evolves rapidly, and what works today might not work tomorrow. But the underlying principles of finding underserved markets, testing ideas cheaply, and building on your existing strengths remain constant.

This book represents what I've learned so far. I hope it helps you find your own path to sustainable income and greater autonomy over your working life.

Core Principles

These are the principles the book is built on. Not tactics, because tactics expire. Not a system, because systems belong to whoever built them. These are the underlying ideas that hold up regardless of which platform is hot this year or which opportunity everyone is chasing.

Skill arbitrage beats price competition

Competing on price is a race you can't win. There's always someone cheaper. The alternative is finding markets where your existing skills are rare and valued, not because you've invented something new, but because you've applied something familiar to a place where it doesn't usually show up. That gap between common skills and uncommon markets is where the real margins are.

Test the riskiest assumption first, as cheaply as possible

Most people test the easy parts of an idea and leave the hard question for later. Later is when it costs the most. Identify the assumption that the whole thing depends on, the one that, if wrong, makes everything else irrelevant, and find the cheapest way to answer it before you build anything around it.

Own the customer relationship

Platform income isn't your income. It's the platform's income, shared with you while it's convenient. When you own the customer relationship directly, their email, their trust, their habit of coming back to you, no algorithm change or policy update can take that away. Build toward that from day one, even if platforms are how you start.

Diversify across risk profiles, not just income sources

Five income streams that all fail for the same reason isn't diversification. The goal is streams that share enough common skills to reinforce each other, but fail independently, with different platforms, different clients, different market conditions. When one is slow, the others don't automatically follow.

Build assets, not just transactions

Every transaction pays once. An asset, a reputation, a system, a product, a client relationship, keeps paying. The question to ask about any work you take on: am I just completing this task, or am I building something that makes the next task easier, better-paid, or unnecessary? Gig work answers the first question. Business building answers the second.

Ethics is risk management

Unethical businesses require a constant supply of new people who haven't been burned yet. That's an exhausting and fragile model. Businesses built on genuine value compound instead of erode. Satisfied clients refer others, reputation opens doors, and you don't have to keep track of what you've told to whom. Beyond the practical argument, it's also just easier to sleep.

Appendix A: AI Tools That Make You Money

None of what follows matters until you know what you're building. The right AI stack for someone testing a ghostwriting business looks completely different from the right stack for someone building a course or selling physical products. Read this chapter as reference material once you have a direction, not as something to implement before you start.

Every week, there's a new AI tool that promises to "revolutionize your business" or "10x your productivity." The marketing is seductive: write content in seconds, generate perfect graphics instantly, automate all your repetitive tasks. Social media is full of entrepreneurs showing off their latest AI workflows and claiming they've replaced entire teams with software.

Most of this is bullshit. Not because AI tools can't be useful, but because the way most people approach AI tools is completely backwards. They chase shiny objects instead of solving real problems. They collect tools instead of creating value. They optimize workflows instead of optimizing results.

The real money in AI tools isn't in using every new tool that launches. It's in finding a small number of tools that solve expensive problems in your business, then using those tools consistently to improve your efficiency and output quality. It's about enhancing your work, not replacing your thinking.

I use exactly four AI tools regularly, and they've probably increased my income by 40% while reducing my workload by 20%. But I've also wasted hundreds of dollars and dozens of hours testing tools that promised to change everything and delivered nothing but distraction.

Before getting into which tools to use, it's worth naming something the productivity conversation usually skips: AI isn't just a tool you can adopt. It's also a competitive pressure on the income streams you're building. Content that used to require a skilled writer can now be drafted by anyone with a prompt. Basic design work, simple code, routine research: the floor on these is dropping. This doesn't mean those skills are worthless. It means the parts of your work that are commoditizable are becoming more commoditizable faster. The response isn't to panic or to ignore it. It's the same as the response to any market shift: move toward the work that requires judgment, relationships, and specific knowledge that AI can't replicate. Use AI to do the routine parts faster so you can spend more time on the parts that actually differentiate you.

The key is approaching AI tools like any other business investment: with clear criteria for success, realistic expectations about results, and the discipline to abandon tools that don't deliver value.

How AI Can Genuinely Boost Income (Not Replace Real Work)

Let's start with what AI tools can't do. They can't replace expertise, judgment, or client relationships. They can't understand context the way humans can. They can't make strategic decisions or solve complex problems that require real-world knowledge.

AI tools are excellent at handling routine tasks that require pattern recognition and repetition. They're terrible at tasks that require creativity, empathy, or deep understanding of human behavior.

The income boost comes from using AI to handle the routine parts of your work so you can focus on the high-value parts that only humans can do. Writing first drafts so you can focus on editing and strategy. Generating design variations so you can focus on creative direction. Automating research so you can focus on analysis and insights.

Claude for writing assistance. I use Claude (yes, this tool) to help with first drafts, research, and editing suggestions. Not to write for me, but to help me write better and faster. I'll feed Claude a topic and ask for an outline, then write the content myself. I'll give Claude my first draft and ask for feedback on structure and clarity.

The value isn't in having Claude write my content - clients hire me for my thinking and my voice, not for generic AI output. The value is in having a writing partner that can help me organize my thoughts, catch mistakes I miss, and suggest improvements I wouldn't think of.

This saves me about 2-3 hours per writing project, which means I can take on more projects or spend more time on high-value activities like client relationship building. The quality of my work has improved because I have a second set of "eyes" reviewing everything before it goes to clients.

> ★ **Pro Tip:** Use AI tools to enhance your core competencies, not to replace them. Your expertise and judgment are what clients pay for.

Word 365's AI features for editing. The built-in AI editing in Word 365 catches grammar mistakes, suggests style improvements, and helps with tone adjustments. It's not perfect, but it's good enough to catch 80% of the errors I would have missed on my own.

This is valuable for someone with ADHD who tends to miss details during proofreading. Instead of spending 30 minutes meticulously proofreading each piece, I can let Word catch the obvious errors and focus my attention on bigger structural issues.

Leonardo AI for visual content. I use Leonardo AI to create images for blog posts, social media, and marketing materials. Not because AI art is better than human art, but because I'm not an artist and hiring designers for every small visual need would be expensive and time-consuming.

The images aren't masterpieces, but they're good enough for most business purposes. Creating a blog post header image that used to require either design skills I don't have or a $50 freelancer payment now takes 5 minutes and costs nothing beyond the subscription.

Automated transcription for interviews. I use AI transcription tools (usually Otter.ai or Word's built-in transcription) to convert client interviews into text that I can search and reference while writing. This saves hours of manual transcription work per project.

The transcriptions aren't perfect - they miss context and get technical terms wrong - but they're accurate enough to serve as a starting point. I can find quotes quickly, reference topics, and organize information more efficiently than I could working from audio alone.

The key principle: AI tools should save you time on tasks that don't require your unique expertise so you can spend more time on tasks that do require your unique expertise.

Avoiding the "Trying Every New Tool" Syndrome

The biggest trap with AI tools is tool addiction - the compulsive need to try every new tool that launches. It feels productive because you're "staying current with technology," but it's usually a form of procrastination that prevents you from doing work.

I fell into this trap hard during 2023. Every time a new AI tool launched, I'd sign up for the free trial, spend hours learning how it worked, and convince myself it was going to revolutionize my business. I tested dozens of tools: content generators, image creators, video editors, automation platforms, productivity apps.

Most of them ended up unused after the initial excitement wore off. I was spending more time learning new tools than I was spending on client work. My productivity decreased even though I had access to more "productivity" tools than ever before.

> ■ **Danger Zone:** Tool testing can become a form of productive procrastination that feels like work but doesn't generate income.

The problem is that every new tool requires learning time, setup time, and integration time. Even if a tool saves you 10 minutes per week, if it takes 3 hours to learn and set up, you won't break even for 18 weeks. Most tools get abandoned long before they pay for the initial time investment.

Tool addiction is dangerous for ADHD brains because we're attracted to novelty and prone to hyperfocus on interesting but unproductive activities. Learning a new AI tool can trigger hyperfocus that lasts for hours while important work gets ignored.

Set clear criteria before testing any new tool. What problem would this tool solve? How much time or money would solving that problem save? How long would it take to learn the tool well enough to get those benefits? Is this problem important enough to justify the learning investment?

Limit tool testing to periods. I now test new tools only during designated evaluation periods, once per quarter. The rest of the time, I use my existing stack and ignore new tool launches. This prevents tool testing from interfering with work.

Track the real cost of new tools. Don't just consider the subscription price - consider the opportunity cost of learning time, the switching cost of changing workflows, and the cognitive load of maintaining more tools in your stack.

> **▲ Caution:** If you find yourself spending more time optimizing your AI workflow than working, you've probably crossed the line from productivity enhancement into productivity theater.

Use the "one in, one out" rule. Before adding a new tool to your stack, identify which existing tool you'll stop using. This prevents tool accumulation and forces you to make explicit tradeoffs about what's valuable.

Most importantly, remember that tools are means to an end, not ends in themselves. The goal is to make more money, create better work, or save meaningful time. If a tool doesn't clearly contribute to one of those goals, it's probably a distraction.

Building a Minimal, Effective AI Stack

The best AI stack is the smallest one that solves your problems. More tools don't equal more productivity - they usually equal more complexity, more subscriptions, and more cognitive overhead.

My entire AI stack consists of four tools that I use regularly and maybe 2-3 others that I use occasionally. This isn't because I'm a minimalist by philosophy - it's because this combination handles 95% of my AI-assisted tasks without the complexity of managing dozens of different tools.

Core stack: Word 365, Claude, Leonardo AI, Otter.ai. These four tools handle writing assistance, content creation, visual generation, and transcription. They cover the major categories of work I do regularly, and each tool is best-in-class for its use case.

Word 365 I was already paying for as part of Office 365, so the AI features are essentially free. Claude is the most capable writing assistant I've tested, and the conversation interface works better for my ADHD brain than prompt-based tools. Leonardo AI produces the best images for my needs at a reasonable price. Otter.ai integrates well with my interview workflow.

Occasional tools: Grammarly, Canva AI, YouTube transcription. I use these tools sometimes but not regularly enough to consider them core parts of my workflow. Grammarly for final proofing on important documents. Canva AI for social media graphics when Leonardo AI isn't quite right. YouTube's automatic transcription for research videos.

The key is that each tool serves a purpose and works well with the others. I'm not using five different writing assistants or three different image generators. Each tool has a clear role, and I've learned to use it effectively.

★ **Pro Tip:** Master a small set of tools instead of dabbling with many tools. Depth beats breadth when it comes to getting value from AI.

Integration matters more than individual tool quality. The best tool for a task might not be the best tool for your overall workflow. A slightly worse tool that integrates well with your existing systems can be more valuable than a better tool that requires constant context switching.

For example, Word 365's AI writing features aren't as sophisticated as some standalone writing assistants, but they work seamlessly within the document editor I'm already using. I don't have to copy and paste between applications or maintain separate tools for writing and editing.

Stick with tools that have staying power. The AI tool landscape changes rapidly, with new tools launching constantly and existing tools shutting down or pivoting. Build your workflow around tools from companies with strong business models and long-term viability.

Microsoft, Google, and other major tech companies are integrating AI into their existing productivity suites. These integrated features might not be as flashy as standalone tools, but they're more likely to be maintained and improved.

The Difference Between Productivity Tools and Productivity Distractions

Not every tool that claims to boost productivity does. Many tools that feel productive are distractions disguised as efficiency improvements.

Productivity tools solve expensive problems efficiently. They save meaningful time on tasks you do frequently, or they improve the quality of your output in ways that clients notice and value. The benefits are measurable and significant relative to the cost and complexity of using the tool.

Productivity distractions create the illusion of progress without meaningful impact. They're fun to use and make you feel like you're optimizing your workflow, but they don't solve problems that matter to your business or income.

I spent weeks testing AI-powered project management tools that promised to revolutionize how I organize my work. The tools were impressive from a technology standpoint - they could categorize tasks automatically, predict project timelines, and generate progress reports.

But my project management "problem" wasn't complex enough to require AI solutions. I have 3-5 clients at any time, with clearly defined projects and deadlines. A simple task list and calendar work perfectly well. The AI project management tools added complexity without adding value.

> ■ **Danger Zone:** Beware of tools that solve problems you don't have. The most sophisticated solution isn't always the most valuable solution.

Real productivity tools have clear ROI. You can calculate how much time or money they save and compare that to their cost. If transcription software saves me 2 hours per project and I do 8 projects per month, it saves 16 hours monthly. At my hourly rate, that's easily worth a $20/month subscription.

Productivity distractions have vague benefits. They promise to "optimize your workflow" or "streamline your process" without measurable improvements. You can't calculate ROI because the benefits are too abstract to quantify.

Real productivity tools integrate into existing workflows. They make current processes faster or better without requiring you to learn entirely new ways of working. You can adopt them gradually and see immediate benefits.

Productivity distractions require workflow overhauls. They promise that if you completely change how you work, you'll be much more productive. But the transition cost is high, and the benefits often don't materialize because the tools don't fit your work patterns.

The test is simple: after using a tool for a month, can you point to measurable improvements in your work output or efficiency? If not, it's probably a distraction masquerading as a productivity tool.

Workflows That Stick vs. Shiny Object Syndrome

The difference between tools that enhance your income and tools that drain your attention is whether you integrate them into sustainable workflows or chase them as shiny objects.

Sustainable workflows solve real problems in your work. They address bottlenecks that genuinely slow you down or quality issues that clients notice. They fit naturally into how you already work without requiring major changes to your process.

Shiny object workflows solve theoretical problems or create solutions in search of problems. They're based on what might be possible instead of what's needed. They require changing how you work to accommodate the tool instead of changing tools to accommodate your work.

My ghostwriting workflow has remained basically the same for three years, but I've gradually integrated AI tools into steps where they add clear value:

Client interview → Otter.ai transcription → Claude-assisted outline → Manual writing → Word 365 AI proofing → Client delivery

Each AI tool slotted into an existing workflow step without changing the overall process. I didn't redesign my workflow around the tools - I found tools that improved my existing workflow.

Start with your current workflow and identify pain points. Don't start with AI tools and try to figure out how to use them. Start with problems in your current work and see if AI tools can solve them efficiently.

What takes too long? What do you avoid doing because it's boring or difficult? What errors do you make repeatedly? What tasks require skills you don't have? These are candidates for AI assistance.

Test tools in your work, not in artificial scenarios. Don't test AI writing tools by asking them to write generic blog posts about common topics. Test them by asking them to help with the type of writing you do for clients.

The test environment should match your real work environment as closely as possible. Use your data, your deadlines, your quality standards. Tools that work well in artificial tests often fail in real-world conditions.

> **⚠ Caution:** Beware of tool vendors who demonstrate their tools using perfect scenarios that don't match the messy reality of client work.

Integrate tools gradually, one at a time. Don't try to revolutionize your entire workflow overnight. Add one tool, use it until it becomes automatic, then consider adding another tool. This prevents workflow chaos and makes it easier to identify which tools provide value.

Measure results, not activities. Don't measure success by how many AI tools you're using or how sophisticated your workflow looks. Measure success by whether you're producing better work, serving clients more efficiently, or increasing your income.

Clients don't care what tools you use. They care about the results you deliver. AI tools are valuable only to the extent that they help you deliver better results more efficiently. Everything else is just expensive procrastination.

The best AI workflow is the one that makes you more money while requiring less effort. If your AI tools aren't clearly contributing to both of those goals, you're probably using them wrong.

Appendix B: The Hardware and Software Stack That Matters

Your setup is only worth thinking about once you know what you're building. A ghostwriter needs different things than a graphic designer or a virtual assistant, and all of them need less than the productivity industry wants you to believe. Read this chapter when you're ready to optimize, not before you've validated that you have something worth optimizing.

The productivity YouTube rabbit hole is deep and expensive. One day you're watching a video about "desk setups that boost productivity," and three hours later you're convinced you need a $300 mechanical keyboard, three 4K monitors, and a standing desk that costs more than most people's cars.

The tech industry has convinced people that the right gear will transform them into productivity machines. Buy this laptop and you'll work faster. Install this app and you'll never miss a deadline. Upgrade to this monitor setup and you'll finally achieve work-life balance.

It's all bullshit designed to separate you from your money.

The truth is that most successful freelancers use surprisingly basic setups. They've figured out that productivity comes from doing the right work efficiently, not from having the most impressive gear. They spend money on tools that solve real problems, not tools that make them feel professional.

Your tech stack should be invisible. When it's working correctly, you don't think about it - you just work. When you spend more time optimizing your setup than working, you've missed the point entirely.

The Minimalist Approach to Tech Setup

I know people making six figures using nothing but a five-year-old laptop and a decent internet connection. I also know people with $5,000 desk setups who can't seem to make $500 a month. The gear isn't the limiting factor - the person using the gear is.

The minimalist approach isn't about being cheap or refusing to invest in your business. It's about being intentional. Every piece of technology in your setup should solve a problem or remove a bottleneck that's preventing you from making money.

Start with what you have. Most people already own the basic tools they need to get started: a computer with internet access. Everything else is optimization, and optimization only matters if you have something worth optimizing.

> ★ **Pro Tip:** Before buying any new tech, ask yourself: "What specific problem will this solve, and how much money will solving that problem make me?"

The productivity porn trap is real. Social media is full of "workspace tours" and "desk setup reveals" that make people think they need elaborate setups to be productive. These setups look impressive in photos, but they're often optimized for aesthetics rather than actual work.

I've visited the home offices of several successful freelancers, and most of them are surprisingly basic. Good lighting, comfortable chair, reliable computer, fast internet. That's it. No RGB lighting, no motorized desks, no walls of monitors. Just functional setups that don't get in the way of work.

The people with the most elaborate setups are usually the ones making the least money. They're spending time and money on gear instead of focusing on finding clients and delivering results. They're treating their setup like a hobby instead of a business investment.

Build around your actual work, not your theoretical needs. If you're a writer, you need a good keyboard and screen. If you're a graphic designer, you need color-accurate monitors and a graphics tablet. If you're doing video calls with clients, you need decent audio and video quality.

But most of this work doesn't require specialized equipment. Customer service, virtual assistance, data entry, social media management, basic writing - these can all be done effectively with standard consumer hardware.

Software That Pays for Itself vs. Software That Drains Your Wallet

The software subscription economy is designed to extract maximum money from users while providing minimum value. Every company wants to convert their one-time purchase into a monthly fee, regardless of whether the subscription model benefits users.

Office 365 vs. Google Workspace vs. free alternatives depends on your client requirements and collaboration needs. If your clients use Microsoft Office, you probably need Office 365 to ensure compatibility. If your clients use Google tools, Google Workspace makes sense. If you work mostly alone, free alternatives like LibreOffice might be sufficient.

I pay for Office 365 because most of my clients use Microsoft tools, and document compatibility problems cost more time and money than the subscription fee. But I wouldn't pay for it if I were just writing for myself or working with clients who use other tools.

When to pay for premium software: when the premium features solve problems that cost you time or money. When free is fine: when the basic features meet your needs and upgrading wouldn't improve your output or efficiency.

Cloud storage that doesn't break the bank means choosing based on your actual usage rather than theoretical maximums. Most people vastly overestimate how much cloud storage they need. Documents and spreadsheets take up almost no space. Images and videos are larger, but most freelancers aren't storing massive media libraries.

I pay for 1TB of OneDrive storage as part of Office 365, which is more than enough for years of documents, client files, and business records. People who pay for multiple cloud storage services or massive storage plans they don't use are wasting money on peace of mind they don't need.

Avoiding subscription creep requires regular audits of what you're paying for and whether you're getting value. Set a calendar reminder to review all subscriptions quarterly. Cancel anything you haven't used in the last month unless you have a clear plan for using it soon.

★ **Pro Tip:** Track all your software subscriptions in a spreadsheet with cost, last used date, and value assessment. You'll be shocked how much you're spending on software you've forgotten about.

The subscription model tricks people into thinking small monthly fees are insignificant, but they add up quickly. Five $10/month subscriptions cost $600 per year.

If those subscriptions don't generate at least $600 in additional income or save $600 worth of time, they're not worth it.

Finding Apps That Work for You (Not Just What's Popular)

The most recommended apps aren't necessarily the best apps for your specific needs and working style. App recommendations are often based on features rather than usability, or they're influenced by affiliate relationships and marketing budgets.

Testing methodology for evaluating tools: start with the free version or trial period. Use the app for actual work, not artificial test scenarios. Track whether the app makes you more productive or just gives you more features to fidget with.

Don't test multiple similar apps simultaneously. Test one app for a week or two, then move to the next one if the first doesn't work out. Parallel testing creates confusion and prevents you from learning any app well enough to judge its effectiveness.

Browser extensions that matter are few but powerful. uBlock Origin blocks ads and trackers that slow down browsing and distract from work. A good password manager (Bitwarden, 1Password) eliminates the time waste and security risk of remembering passwords. Productivity blockers (Cold Turkey, StayFocusd) prevent access to distracting websites during work hours.

Most other browser extensions are solutions in search of problems. They add complexity and potential security risks without meaningful benefits. If you have more than

5-6 browser extensions installed, you probably have more than you need.

Antivirus reality check: Windows Defender is adequate for most users who practice basic security hygiene. Third-party antivirus software often creates more problems than it solves - slowing down systems, generating false positives, and nagging users with upgrade prompts.

If you're handling sensitive client data or working in high-risk industries, enterprise antivirus solutions might be necessary. But most freelancers and gig workers are better served by Windows Defender plus good backup practices than by resource-heavy security suites.

Email clients, file managers, and other "boring" tools make or break daily productivity. The default apps (Windows Mail, File Explorer) work fine for basic needs, but power users benefit from more capable alternatives (Thunderbird, Directory Opus).

The key is choosing tools that match your usage patterns rather than tools with the most features. If you send 50 emails per day, a powerful email client is worth the learning curve. If you send 5 emails per day, the default client is probably fine.

Essential Services Worth Paying For

Some services are worth paying for because the free alternatives create more problems than they solve, or because the cost of failure is higher than the cost of the service.

Backblaze and other "set it and forget it" backup solutions are insurance policies. You hope you'll never need them, but when your hard drive fails or your laptop gets stolen, they're worth far more than their cost.

I use Backblaze for unlimited cloud backup ($60/year) and local backup to an external drive. The cloud backup handles catastrophic failures like theft or fire. The local backup handles quick restores for individual files or minor hardware problems.

> ■ **Danger Zone:** "I'll back up my files later" is how people lose years of work. Set up automated backups before you need them.

Web hosting and domain registrars that don't suck means choosing companies that will still exist in five years and won't hold your domain hostage with transfer fees and complicated processes.

For domain registration, Namecheap and Porkbun are reliable and reasonably priced. Avoid GoDaddy - they're expensive and make domain transfers unnecessarily difficult. For web hosting, if you need a simple website, shared hosting from companies like SiteGround or A2 Hosting works fine.

If you're just starting out and don't need a custom website, free options like GitHub Pages or platform-specific sites (LinkedIn, Upwork profiles) might be sufficient. But having your own domain and basic website becomes important as you establish your professional brand.

Internet service providers: when to pay more for reliability depends on how much money you lose when your internet goes down. If a few hours of downtime costs you hundreds of dollars in lost work or client frustration, business-grade internet with better uptime guarantees might be worth the extra cost.

For most gig workers, residential internet is adequate as long as it's fast enough for video calls and file uploads. But having a backup connection (mobile hotspot, secondary provider) is cheap insurance against outages.

Phone and data plans for people who work from anywhere need to balance cost with reliability. If you're often in areas with poor cell coverage, paying more for a carrier with better coverage is a business expense, not a luxury.

I use a mainstream carrier with unlimited data because I sometimes work from coffee shops or client offices where WiFi isn't available. The extra cost is less than what I'd lose from missed calls or inability to access client files.

Banking and financial tools for freelancers need to separate business and personal finances without creating administrative overhead. A separate business checking account is usually sufficient - you don't need complex business banking packages unless you're handling large volumes of transactions.

For accounting, simple tools like Wave (free) or QuickBooks Simple Start ($15/month) handle invoicing and expense tracking for most solo operations. Complex accounting software is overkill unless you have employees or complicated business structures.

Cost-Benefit Analysis of Tech Investments

Every tech purchase should be evaluated as a business investment with expected returns, not as a consumer purchase based on wants or status.

Calculating ROI on hardware purchases: how much time will this save, how much additional income will this enable, how much will this reduce current expenses? If a faster computer saves 2 hours per week, what's your hourly rate worth over the useful life of the computer?

A $1,500 computer that saves 2 hours per week for someone billing $50/hour pays for itself in 15 weeks. A $500 computer that saves 1.5 hours per week pays for itself in 7 weeks. The cheaper computer might be the better investment even if the expensive computer is "better."

When upgrades pay for themselves: when current technology creates bottlenecks that cost time or money, when reliability problems cause missed deadlines or client frustration, when hardware limitations prevent you from taking on better-paying work.

When upgrades are just wants: when current technology works fine but newer technology has attractive features, when upgrades are motivated by what others have rather than actual problems, when the cost exceeds the realistic income benefit.

I upgraded my laptop when the old one started freezing during video calls with clients. The upgrade cost $1,200 but prevented embarrassing technical problems that could cost client relationships. That's a clear business justification.

But I haven't upgraded my monitors in five years because they work fine for my needs. Newer monitors have better colors and higher resolution, but better colors wouldn't increase my income or improve my work quality for writing-focused projects.

The true cost of "cheap" solutions includes the time cost of dealing with problems, the opportunity cost of reduced productivity, and the replacement cost when cheap solutions fail sooner.

A $300 laptop that needs to be replaced every two years costs more than a $800 laptop that lasts four years. A $50 office chair that causes back pain costs more than a $200 chair that's comfortable for long work sessions.

But expensive doesn't always mean better value. A $2,000 laptop that offers minimal improvements over a $800 laptop is bad value even if it lasts longer. Paying for features you don't need or performance you won't use is waste, not investment.

Your tech stack should scale with your income. Start with good enough solutions and upgrade when business growth justifies better tools. Don't buy the tools you'll need when you're making $10,000/month if you're currently making $1,000/month.

Start with the minimum viable setup for your current income level. Invest in upgrades when current limitations prevent growth, not in anticipation of growth that might not happen.

Your tech stack should be a business tool that enables income generation, not a hobby that consumes income. Every purchase should make you more productive, more professional, or more capable of serving clients effectively.

When your tech fades into the background and just works, you've built the right setup. When you spend more time thinking about your tech than using it productively, you've probably overthought the problem.

The best setup is the one that lets you focus on your work instead of your tools.

Books by Richard Lowe

See books by Richard Lowe at
https://masterofworlds.com

Get free publishing insights and industry updates at
https://thewritingking.substack.com

For ghostwriting and book coaching services see
https://thewritingking.com